ME and MINE

Helen Sekaquaptewa   *Photograph by Robert R. Lewis*

ME and MINE

The Life Story of Helen Sekaquaptewa

as told to Louise Udall

Illustrated by Phillip Sekaquaptewa

THE UNIVERSITY OF ARIZONA PRESS
Tucson & London

Ninth printing 1991
The University of Arizona Press

This book was set in 12/13 Linotype Monticello

Copyright © 1969
The Arizona Board of Regents
All Rights Reserved
Manufactured in the U.S.A.

∞ This book is printed on acid-free, archival-quality paper.

ISBN 0-8165-0270-6
LC No. 68-54714

To my husband, Emory Sekaquaptewa
and to our children
and to our children's children

— HELEN

How the story came to be written

MY FRIENDSHIP WITH HELEN began when she was living in Phoenix, keeping a home for her children who were attending high school and college. Once every week she rode with me, out southwest of Phoenix to the Maricopa Reservation where we spent the afternoon holding Relief Society meetings (the women's organization of the Church of Jesus Christ of Latter-Day Saints) with the Maricopa Indians. As we traveled we visited.

The many things she told me about her life prompted me to say, "You should write the story of your life for your children and grandchildren."

Her answer was, "I have thought of doing it, but didn't think I was capable."

I started writing the events as she told them. I visited her at the Ranch for weeks at a time, and the story grew and grew.

The Trader at Oraibi asked, "What is Mrs. Udall writing? I know she is writing something."

Helen replied, "I am talking. She is writing."

LOUISE UDALL

CONTENTS

Childhood	3
The Well	17
Kachinvaki	23
Emory's Early Years	30
Food, Clothing, and Shelter	36
Barter and Trade	55
The Line	63
The Aftermath	85
To School in Keams Canyon	91
Home for One Year	109
Back to School	121
Phoenix Indian School	132
Home after Thirteen Years	144
Marriage	153
Idaho, Here We Come	167
Hotevilla	174
The Ranch	197
My Church	224
Dasube	245
In Retrospect	251
Index	257

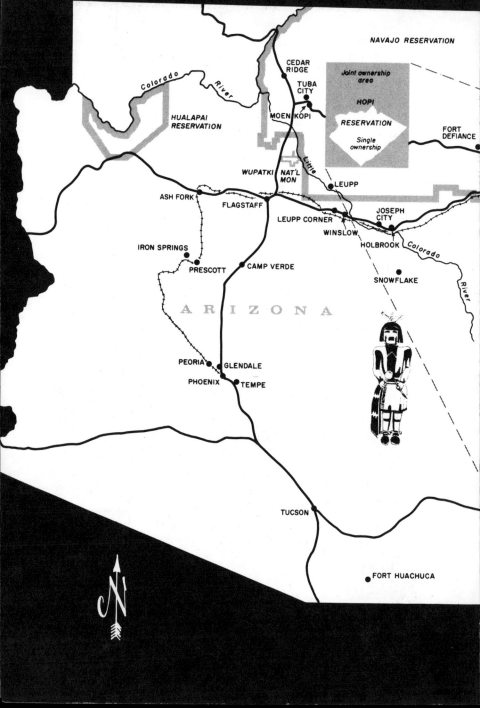

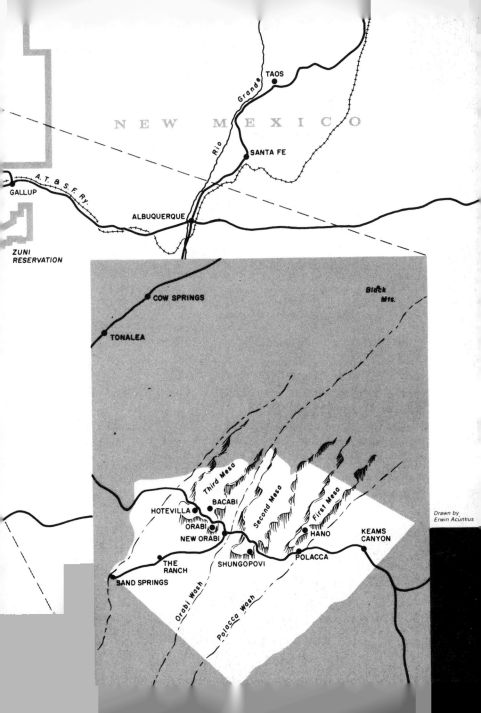

Who can find a virtuous woman? for her price
is far above rubies.

The heart of her husband doth safely
trust in her, . . .

She will do him good and not evil all the days
of her life.

She seeketh wool and flax, and worketh
willingly with her hands.

She riseth also while it is yet night, and giveth
meat to her household.

She stretcheth out her hands to the poor; yea,
she reacheth forth her hands to the needy.

Strength and honor are her clothing; and
she shall rejoice in time to come.

She openeth her mouth with wisdom; and in
her tongue is the law of kindness.

Her children arise up, and call her blessed;
her husband also, and he praiseth her.

Give her the fruit of her hands; and let her
own works praise her in the gates.

Proverbs–31: 10–13, 15, 20, 25, 26, 28, 31

ME and MINE

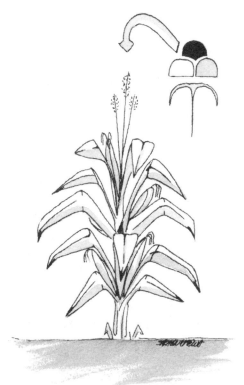

Childhood

MY HOMELAND is the arid, sandy, plateau country of northeastern Arizona, where dwell the
Hopi people in eleven villages, each with similar
characteristics and mores, yet each a separate
city-state, and not always on friendly terms with
the neighbors.

My village, Oraibi (oh-ryé-bee), known to
have been inhabited continuously since the time
of Columbus, was built at the end of a mesa that
juts out like a promontory and narrows where

it joins the tableland. The site was selected for security and ease in defense. On three sides were steep and rocky cliffs, with one or two possible access trails, making it possible for a few men to stand off an invasion.

Hopis say, "The sun has so much work to do, warming the whole earth and making things grow. Do not add to his burden by making him have to get you up. Get up before the sun comes up." Older men should be on the roof in time to watch the sun rise. Able-bodied men and the youth, prodded by their uncles' get-up call to "Come on and take a run out to the water," would dash cold water all over their naked bodies and run back to the village, to build strong and healthy bodies. Every man knew that he had to have a strong body to be able to defend himself and his home and his village. Even after working hard all day, a Hopi man spent time shooting with bows and arrows and doing exercises to strengthen all his muscles, especially those of the arms and hands. He must be able to draw a tight bow and shoot an arrow swift and straight. Everyone watched for signs of raiders, especially at harvest time.

In every village there are as many kivas as there are societies.* The kiva is a good-sized

---

* A society is made up of members from clans associated together for a specific purpose — such as the Warriors Society for defense.

room, partly underground, the entrance being from the top by ladder. It is many things; it has sacred and ceremonial use and also provides a sort of club room, a school room, and a religious and community center for the male members of the specific society. The men may gather there during the winter mornings just to visit and get warm while their wives are getting breakfast ready. The robes for the brides are woven in the kiva. The snake priests perform the greater part of their ceremonial prayer for rain in their kiva. In winter evenings the men go to the kiva, taking their sons with them to learn and practice ceremonial songs and dances, and to retell their traditional stories and give moral and civic training. A high standard of dignity and decorum is religiously maintained.

Hopi legend tells that long ago the kachinas (messengers from the gods) came and delivered instructions and admonitions in person, mingling with the people in the ceremonial dances. When the kachinas ceased to come, the priests put on masks and costumes and impersonated the different ones. The priest assumes the authority and character of, and "becomes," that kachina, and due respect is given him as such. Although all adults know that the kachina is a man with a mask, they respect and obey this representative of deity. There are many kachinas, each with his own distinctive costume and mission.

Masks and costumes are stored in the kivas when not in use.

My mother, Sehynim, was raised by her grandparents, Beecho and Qumanimka. Beecho, being anxious that his granddaughter marry a man who would husband well the many flocks and herds which she would bring him, when Sehynim was of marriageable age, selected a young man whom he knew to be a hard worker and who would take good care of lands and stock. He saw that the marriage took place. My father, Talashonga, when he learned that his marriage had been fixed, was sort of offended. He did not go to claim his bride for a long time and then stayed only a few days at a time. As time passed, they loved each other and were happy together.

My mother inherited quite a lot of jewelry, which had been in the family for a long time — strings of turquoise and coral and beads made from sea shells. Turquoise is found in our area, but the coral and shells came from the Pacific coast, hundreds of miles away. These were trade items and show that merchandising extended afar. The shells are broken into little pieces and a hole drilled in the center of each. Then they are strung on a string or stick, and shaped and polished by twirling against a sandstone.

I was born in Old Oraibi in 1898. When I

was twenty days old I was taken by my mother and my paternal grandmother to the eastern edge of the mesa. There, in accord with Hopi custom, as the sun came up, they petitioned to him to take notice of this little Hopi girl baby and bless her with life, health, and a family. Several names were given me, one of which "took" and became my name, Dowawisnima (dew-wow-iss-nima), which means a "trail marked by sand."

The house where I was born stood for years on the northwest edge of Old Oraibi mesa. The house was torn down and the timbers re-used in other houses, but the earliest memories of my life there still live in my heart. There was love in my home, and I felt happy and secure during my childhood. I began learning about life just like all children do, from imitating my elders. My mother seemed to be grinding corn most of the time. Little girls all over the village played at grinding corn. When I was about five years old my mother put me on a real grinding stone along-side her, with a few kernels of corn, and let me grind a little while. This corn, my initial grind-ings, she fed to the chickens.

I spent many happy hours playing pleasant games with other children in the village plaza. Sometimes we even ventured out among the rocks and cedar trees in games of chase and hide-and-seek.

By the time I was old enough to go to school,

there had been a day school built down off the mesa, where children up to the third grade could go to school by day and live at home. This was a concession to the Hopi parents, but still, many of them resisted even putting their children into the day school.

When we were five or six years of age, we, with our parents (Hostiles) became involved with the school officials, assisted by the Navajo policemen, in a serious and rather desperate game of hide-and-seek, where little Hopi boys and girls were the forfeit in the game. Every day the school principal sent out a truant officer, and many times he himself went with the officer, going to Hopi homes to take the children to school. The Navajo policemen who assisted in finding hidden children were dressed in old army uniforms, and they wore regular cavalry hats over their long hair, done up in a knot. This made quite a picture — especially the traditional hair style with a white man's hat. It had not been customary for Indians to wear hats up to that time.

When September came there was no peace for us. Early in the morning, from our houses on the mesa, we could see the principal and the officer start out from the school, walking up the trail to "get" the children. Hostile parents tried every day in different ways to hide us from them, for once you were caught, you had lost the game.

You were discovered and listed and you had to go to school and not hide any more. I was finally caught and went to the Oraibi day school one session, when I was about six years old, but not before many times outwitting Mr. Schoolman.

Sometimes, after a very early breakfast, somebody's grandmother would take a lunch and go with a group of eight to twelve little girls and hide them in the cornfields away out from the village. On another day another grandmother would go in the other direction over the hills among the cedars where we would play in a ravine, have our lunch and come back home in the afternoon. Men would be out with little boys playing this game of hide and seek. One day I got left behind and was sent out with a group of boys. I didn't know the man, and the boys' games were not for me, and I cried all day.

A place where one or two small children could be stowed away on short notice was the rabbit blanket. A rabbit blanket is made by cutting dressed rabbit skins in two-inch strips and weaving them into a warp of wool thread. When not in use, in warm weather, this blanket is hung by the four corners from a hook in the rafter beam, to prevent it from being moth-eaten. But once discovered, this hiding place was out. The school officer would feel of the rabbit blanket first thing on coming into the room.

Most houses have a piki storage cupboard in

a partition wall. This would be the thickness of the wall and about two by three feet. A cloth covered the front, making a good place to keep the piki supply dry and clean. One day the officers were only two doors away when my mother was aware of their presence. She snatched her young son Henry and put him curled up in the piki cupboard just in time to win the game — that day.

Our houses were two and three stories high. When a lower room became old and unsafe, it was used as a dump place for ashes, peach stones, melon and squash seeds, and bits of discarded corn; anything that could be eaten was preserved in the ashes, and the room was gradually filled. Then in time of famine these bits of food could be dug out and eaten. In the home of my childhood such a room was about three-fourths filled. One September morning my brother and I were hidden there. We lay on our stomachs in the dark, facing a small opening. We saw the feet of the principal and policeman as they walked by, and heard their big voices as they looked about wondering where the children were. They didn't find us that day.

One morning an older man took several boys out to hide. Emory, who later was my husband, was one of these boys. The man took them off the mesa where there was a big fissure in a sheer cliff with a bigger space behind it, away down in the rocks where no horse could go. The grandfather told the boys to stay there and be quiet. He then went a little way away and began hoeing in an orchard. The boys soon wanted to come out and play, but the grandfather said "no." Pretty soon they heard the sound of approaching horses' hoofs and looking up to the top of the cliff saw the Navajo policeman. He rode around out of sight, but pretty soon was seen coming up the valley toward the grandfather. The policeman couldn't get into the crack in the rock but he got off his horse looking for footprints. The boys had been careful to step on rocks and grass and left no footprints. After looking around a while the policeman got on his horse and rode away. After he left and they were sure he would not come back, then the boys came out to play, and later the grandfather brought out the lunch.

Some boys made trouble after they were enrolled in school. At recess they would run away. They could outrun the principal. One principal, in desperation, got himself a .22 rifle with blank bullets. When he shot at the boys they stopped running.

I don't remember for sure just how I came to be "caught." Maybe both my mother and myself got a little tired of getting up early every morning and running off to hide all day. She probably thought to herself, "Oh, let them get her. I am tired of this. It is wearing me down." The hide-and-seek game continued through September, but with October, the colder weather was on the schoolman's side.

So, one morning, I was "caught." Even then, it was the rule among mothers not to let the child go voluntarily. As the policeman reached to take me by the arm, my mother put her arm around me. Tradition required that it appear that I was forced into school. I was escorted down off the mesa to the schoolhouse, along with several other children. First, each was given a bath by one of the Indian women who worked at the school. Baths were given in the kitchen in a round, galvanized tub. Then we were clothed in cotton underwear, cotton dresses, and long black stockings and heavy shoes, furnished by the government. Each week we had a bath and a complete change of clothing. We were permitted to wear the clothes home each day, but my mother took off the clothes of the detested white man as soon as I got home, until it was time to go to school the next day.

Names were given to each child by the school. Mine was "Helen." Each child had a name card pinned on, for as many days as it took for the teacher to learn and remember the name she had given us. Our teacher was Miss Stanley. She began by teaching us the names of objects about the room. We read a little from big charts on the wall later on, but I don't remember ever using any books.

A feud developed over the years as the people were divided into sides for and against those who came from the outside. These two factions were known as the "Friendlies" (to the government) and the "Hostiles" (to the government), and "they" came to mean anyone who represented an outside influence. Later these groups were known as the "Progressives" and the "Traditionals."

Those who put their children into school voluntarily were given an ax, a hoe, a shovel, or a rake, but stoves and wagons they had to work for. Hostile parents scornfully rejected these tools even though they would have served them better than the implements they made of wood or stone. These overtures were looked upon only as a bait or wedge that would end in no good to them. Hostile parents warned their children, when they were leaving for school, "Don't take the pencil in your hand. If you do, it means you give consent to what they want you to do. Don't do it."

The attitude of the parents carried over to their children, as was shown on the schoolgrounds. The children of the "Friendlies" made fun of us, calling us "Hostiles," and they would not let us join with them in their play, so I was unhappy some of the time. However, I do have pleasant memories of how one of my fourteen-year-old cousins used to carry me on his back down off the mesa to school. Going back up the trail after school was often a skirmish. My older brother would carefully lead his little sister up the trails going home. The "Friendly" children often ran ahead up the trail and gathered rocks and threw them down at us when we came to the bottom of the steep rocky ledge. Sometimes we would try another way up, following little gullies, or going around and coming up on the trail on the opposite side of the mesa — the long way home — to avoid being pelted with rocks.

I liked school. It was pleasant and warm inside. I liked to wear the clothes they gave us at school; but when I learned that the kids were "hostile" to us, I didn't want to go to school. Everyone, even the principal and the teachers and employees, were more or less against us.

The Mennonites had a church in Old Oraibi, but our parents would not let us go even to their Sunday School. We wanted to go, and sometimes we went around the mesa and came to Sunday School by a back path. They would give us a little ticket each time we came, and on Christmas they gave a big prize to the one who had the most tickets. We did not understand much that they said, but it was nice to be there. I received a few tickets but gave them away. I did not dare to accept a present.

Each little Hopi girl had her family of bone dolls, which she collected and hoarded and treasured, keeping them in a little sack or a baking powder can with a lid, whatever container she could come by. These bones came from the lower parts of the legs of the sheep. A two-inch was the man doll. A smaller one was the woman. The same bones from smaller animals were the children. Chickens were triangular-shaped bones from the horny hoof. When the sheep was slaughtered, the last four inches of the legs were singed, scraped, and cleaned white, and used to flavor a pot of boiled hominy, thus making it rich in glutinous protein. The Hopis knew it was good because it tasted good. As a member of the family ate clean such a bone, it would be given to the little girl, as is done with the wishbone from a chicken or turkey. After the bone was dried in the sun, it was white and pretty like ivory.

Hours could be spent with bone dolls, either alone or in groups. Sometimes the girls brought their dolls to school and would play with them at recess out in the yard. Since I was not included in the play, I liked to stand near enough to listen and watch, but when they discovered what I was doing they would drive me away.

First the girls gathered little flat rocks, then they smoothed the sand and used the rocks to mark off a house, partition the rooms, and make the furniture. One certain bone was the broom. With it the floor was marked, leaving a waffle-like pattern in the sand. A chicken yard was enclosed and the chickens put in their places. An old discolored bone was the grandmother, set surrounded with children or tending the baby.

With the stage all set, the little girl reenacted family life, speaking for the characters, cooking, feeding, training her children, and as the day ended putting them to bed. There would be a quiet time; then, a cock would crow, the chickens would begin to talk, and the mother would get the family started on another day. The girls had boundless imagination as they dramatically portrayed real life.

A little bone doll boy might go outside the village to play and come running back to report, "There is a big giant coming." The giant idea probably came from seeing a big bone. Whereupon the father bone would come out to defend his home. A fight ensued as the two clashed in the hands of the little girl, and the father would put the intruder to flight. Bone women gossiped and discussed their families and neighbors.

The Well

SOME OF THE EARLIEST of my childhood memories center about the well at Old Oraibi. It is situated down off the mesa about a mile away, via a well-worn trail, and — as in the old Bible days — was for many, many years the sole source of water for the village. Water was scarce and therefore precious. The well itself, dug long, long ago, before the use of pulley or pump, is at the bottom of a basin about one hundred feet or more in diameter and thirty-five feet deep. The soil is very sandy. At the bottom, where the water stands, there is a retaining wall of piled-up rock about four and one-half feet in height that holds back the sand, except on one side where stone steps lead down from the top of the well. A series of four rock-lined terraces, each about five feet wide, widens gradually out to the rim of the basin. Water seeps slowly into the well.

On any day fifty years ago, or one hundred, or five hundred years ago, a two-to-five-gallon earthen water jug sat on each stone step. Sometimes the line of water jugs extended up and beyond the top level of the basin and back up the sandy path toward the village.

Carrying water was the task of the older women. Each put her jar in place in the line and retired to the surface to await her turn. When there was enough water to fill a jar, the owner first in line went down and dipped the water into her jug with a gourd. As she moved out, the next woman in line moved her jar and everyone moved one step closer to the well. Sometimes one might save herself the effort by calling to a friend, "Move mine up too."

The water vessel is made of pottery with one side flattened to fit the back; it is narrow at the neck to prevent spilling and has two handles by which it is carried up the steps. The woman set her filled jar in the center of a large piece of fabric — usually an old discarded, well-darned dress — and folded the two opposite corners (bias) over it; next she tied the remaining two corners in a knot. She now hoisted the load to her back with the knotted ends resting on her forehead or chest, and started up the trail to the village. In summer the woman pulled a green weed and at rest intervals dropped the weed to the ground, stepping on it to cool her bare feet. Once home, she emptied her water into a larger storage vessel and returned to the well to get in line again. When the flow was low, in June and July, this went on day and night. A woman might take two jars and tell her husband to come on down by the time they were filled and carry one jar for her.

A good shelter and shade where the ladies could sit and sew or darn or gossip to pass away the time was made by stretching blankets over and between the big sand rocks close by. In summertime the water carrier might sleep there on the ground during the night hours that she waited. Usually a woman would wait for another so they could climb the path together in the dark.

There was a time for big girls to carry water too. This was more of a social affair than a necessity. After the girls had finished grinding for the day they would form a party and go late in the afternoon. They walked out of the village in single file with their vessels on their backs. When they were outside the village they could walk in groups visiting and at ease. Jugs made especially for girls were called mon-we-goro, which means "girl jugs." These jugs were shaped like the ones the women carried, but smaller. The girls would go to a smaller spring, farther way from the village, and might not find nor bring any water back. The idea was for relaxation, but it had to appear that they had a purpose.

As children roaming about, we would come to the well, hot and thirsty, and ask for a drink of water. If it was a hard-boiled old woman waiting her turn she would say, "Go home and get a drink." If it was a nice, kindly, old woman she would gladly give us a drink.

Every spring and fall there was a community cleaning of the well. The sand and weeds that had accumulated within the basin had to be cleaned out and carried away. This was important, and several kachinas took charge, going to every house and ordering everyone to report at the well on that day to work. It was their duty. Some young men might run away just for the fun of having the kachinas chase them, but if one refused to go he was whipped hard with yucca branches. No one was excused. Kachinas also ordered all of the women and girls to prepare food and bring it to the well at noon that the workers might eat. On the day before the well cleaning every family got enough water to last for an extra day.

Lines were formed, and as baskets were filled with sand and weeds they were passed from hand to hand, up and out, to be dumped far away from the rim of the basin. Little children would go in and out carrying dirt in whatever container they might have — a basket, a rag, or a can. Even at the very bottom of the well itself, an accumulation of sand was cleaned out and carried away. After this cleaning it took several hours for the sand to settle before the water became clear and ready for use.

Nearly every family had a cistern, a big basin in the sand rock that cropped out all over the mesa, where they caught and stored rain water for a supplementary supply. When there was snow, they would pile it up and pack it around their cistern as high as six feet so that as the snow melted the water would run into the cistern. The biggest cisterns were made during the time of the Catholic Priests (1560-1680), because they had better tools. These cisterns were claimed by the village chiefs. Each family guarded its cistern jealously, and there were sometimes big fights over this water.

Every drop of water was precious, and there was never enough. From infancy we were taught to drink sparingly; even then, there were times when we were always thirsty. You never asked for a drink when visiting at a neighbor's house but went home to drink from your own water. The sheep, cattle, horses, and burros were watered at the Hotevilla springs, six miles away. There was concern about the future of the village. Were the water supply to diminish and the population increase, what would become of the people? A prophecy that there would come a time when the village would be divided and some of the people forced to migrate seemed to offer a solution.

The well has not been used for half a century now. Sand has blown in and piled up on the terraces, and they are grown up with weeds. Some of the retaining walls have collapsed, and some of the sandstone steps are washed away, and the old well is abandoned and forgotten.

The government drilled wells when they built schools down off the mesa at New Oraibi. They set up tanks and piped water into the buildings. There are several places about the town where water is on tap. Up at Old Oraibi, they haul their water in cans by wagons or trucks from New Oraibi wells.

Kachinvaki

KACHINVAKI IS THE first ceremony in which
Hopi children participate, being the initiatory
step into a society; it is also called "The Whipping." It is in the nature of a baptism — that is,
to drive out the "bad." It occurs in the spring of
each year in connection with the Bean Dance.
All children who have reached the age of seven
or eight during the past year take part in Kachinvaki.

Little children are told that the kachinas are

magic and come from their home in the San Francisco Peaks to take part in the various ceremonials. Children too young to be initiated are not permitted to go to the night performances, so they don't discover that the kachina is only a man with a costume and a mask. In the daytime part of the dance, little children may watch, but from far off so they won't guess.

When I was the right age my mother chose a woman to be my godmother. My mother gave me a little white cornmeal in my hand and told me to go to a certain woman and ask her to be my godmother and to offer her the cornmeal. I did, and she took the cornmeal; it meant that she would act as my godmother at Kachinvaki and all my life afterward. If she refused it, I was to bring the cornmeal back and try another woman; but she was a kind woman and accepted my offering and was always a good godmother to me. Kachinvaki comes in February, but the godmother is chosen in the summer before to give her time to make a plaque as a gift to her godchild, and for her son or her husband to carve a doll kachina to be presented to the child during the rites in February.

When the day came for Kachinvaki, my mother dressed me in freshly washed clothes. First she wrapped an old belt around my waist, next to my skin. It went around two or three times and I wondered at the time why the two

belts? In late afternoon, about half an hour before we were to go to the kiva, my godmother
came and took me to her house. As we left the
house to go to the kiva she gave me an ear of
corn which I was to hold in my hand all during
the ceremony. My godmother's eldest son went
with us to act as my godfather. Each took hold
of one of my hands as we left the house.

Everyone in the village was out to watch; the
youths were on the housetops watching to see
the Kachinas as they came running into the village and to hear the wild shrieks as the whipping
got under way.

My godparents still held my hands as we
descended the ladder into the kiva; it took us a
long time to take the steps. A man was sitting
at the foot of the ladder holding a hoop about two
and a half feet in diameter, the hoop resting on
the floor. Each child in turn stepped into this
hoop, and the man lifted it up over the child's
body and lowered it four times, ending with the
hoop on the floor. There were thirty or more
children on this day. The kiva floor has two
levels, one-fourth of the area being raised about
one foot. My godmother took her place on the
upper level with the other godmothers, and my
godfather stayed with me on the lower floor.
I was so young and scared that I was in a fog,
but I thought I could see a sort of cloth tent in
one corner of the room and someone in it.

After all the children had come down the ladder and taken their places, a man talked to us for a long time, like a sermon. He is called the "story teller." Talking in a singsong manner, he told us about the kachinas and how they came to be. I could not understand much of what he was saying. Four times during this storytelling, little mudhead kachinas came out from the tent in the corner. They were boys in black kilts with rag masks on their heads with protruding eyes made of balls of cotton wrapped in cloth and painted all over with mud. The upper part of their bodies were painted with pinkish mud. Holding in their hands an ear of corn and some feathers, hands held close together, the mudheads would stop before each child, pass their arms toward the child in a waving motion, and then go back to the tent.

The storyteller told us that the kachinas were coming to initiate us. A man on the roof of the kiva was watching and listening. Another watchman was on a high housetop. The kachinas were watching at the edge of the village. At the proper time, the man on the kiva roof stood up, and this was the signal to the man on the housetop to also stand, and the kachinas knew that it was time to come on the run so as to appear and enter the kiva as the storyteller said, "They are coming, closer. Now they are here." We heard the two whipper kachinas making a lot of noise as they stopped and clanked the turtle shells fastened to their legs. They ran around the kiva four times before coming down the ladder into the kiva. With the whipper kachinas came a mother kachina, carrying in her arms a big bundle of fresh yucca to serve as whips. All the children were afraid, and the timid ones were crying already.

Children of the Badger and the Kachina clans are not whipped; neither are the children whose godfathers are from those clans. Their initiation is Powamoivaki, not Kachinvaki, and takes place two days earlier. However, they are required to attend Kachinvaki. Even these, who stand with the women, were scared and crying too.

The kachinas came in fast and were fierce-looking things. They stood by the fireplace. The first child in line, if it is a boy, has on only a blanket, which his sponsor removes, and he stands in the nude. The godfather takes hold of the hands of the boy and pulls him over in front of the whippers and lifts the arms of the boy above his head, while he receives four hard lashes. If the godfather sees fit, he may pull the boy away and put out his own leg and take one or two lashes for his godson.

It goes fast, with much crying. When a whip gets limp a new one — four yucca branches — is taken. The whippers take turns with the lash, while the mother whipper urges them on, mostly with the boys, saying, "Whip him hard. He is naughty. Don't be lenient with him." Parents may have told her of some naughty thing that the son has done, which she repeats. There are big welts on the backs of the boys and sometimes they are bleeding.

If a little girl is wearing a shawl, her godfather takes it off, takes hold of her hands and leads her over to get whipped, as he holds her hands above her head. I knew then why my mother put two belts on me. The four lashes were given around the waist and it didn't hurt much. The tips of the yucca did give a little sting.

When all had been whipped my godparents each took me by a hand and we climbed the ladder and out of the kiva and went back to my godmother's house where she gave me a comfortable seat and said she would get me something to eat. I was so upset and scared that I didn't eat much of the nice food that she fixed. Then I went home alone.

At sunup three days later the kachinas came again to the homes and gave presents to the children — the woven plaques and dolls made by the godparents, also gifts from parents and aunts of the little initiate. One child might receive as many as ten plaques if she had a lot of aunts. These she could keep or sell, as she chose.

The final event is an all-night dance where the kachinas come and dance; all wear costumes, but some do not wear masks. Other masks are lined up on a shelf, and during the evening all remove their masks so that the children see that it is men and not magic. So now we know. During the dance, all the initiates must sit on a bench with their knees drawn up. They may not hang their feet down at any time. The godmother may step down and get a drink of water for the child, and he is permitted to step outside to relax for a few minutes; otherwise he must stay in that position until the break of day, when the ceremony is finished. At the conclusion, the children are advised that they may now begin to take part in the affairs of the societies; they are admonished not to talk about what they have seen to children who are younger. "If you do tell about this, a lot of kachinas will come and whip you until you are dead."

It was quite an ordeal for me. When I went back to my home I wished I didn't know that a kachina was a man with a costume and a mask, when all the time I had thought they were real magic.

Emory's Early Years

I THINK I SHOULD TELL some of the events in the life of my husband Emory. His father and mother were separated, the father being a Hostile and living in Hotevilla. After 1906, Emory's father, along with others, was sent away for five years to Carlisle Institute in Pennsylvania, where it was hoped they would develop into community leaders. When he came back, he married a woman from Hotevilla. When Emory was little he lived in Oraibi with his mother and stepfather. Emory's grandfather, Wickvaya, was a part of his daughter's household, and he looked after little Emory.

A small boarding school for Hopis was built at Keams Canyon in 1887. At first they took only boys and girls whose parents gave consent, but later the policy changed. When Emory was five years old he was sleeping with his little brothers on the second floor terrace of his home in Old Oraibi. One September morning, early, without his mother's knowledge, the school police took little Emory, still asleep, wrapped in a brand new blanket that his grandfather had made for him. They took him and deposited him in the schoolhouse down at New Oraibi before he was fully awake. He was bewildered and didn't know where he was until he looked out of the window and realized that he was at the schoolhouse. This was Emory's initiation into the white man's way of education. Could we now say that Emory was the original "head start?" The "catch" that day was Emory, another six-year-old boy, and six girls who had not gone back to school after the summer vacation.

Answering the question, "Emory, did your mother come after you when she found that you were gone?" he replied, "No. It wouldn't have done her any good. They wouldn't have let her see me." The two little boys and the girls were

soon loaded into a wagon for the thirty-mile trip
to Keams Canyon. Emory recalls:

*In the middle of the afternoon we passed a
melon patch, and the Navajo police who were
with us brought several of the melons for us to
eat. I don't think the melons belonged to them,
but they tasted good to hungry children. The
girls mothered the little boys.*

*It was after dark when we got to the Canyon,
and the evening meal in the dining room had
been over for hours. We were herded into the
dining room and given hard tack and syrup in
a saucer. The next thing I knew I was in a big
room full of boys and put into a bed. In the morning we were issued regular government clothing
— blue shirt, mustard-colored pants, and heavy
shoes. My beautiful new blanket with colored
stripes was gone. I saw it later, in the possession
of the wife of the superintendent.*

*In 1901, when I first went to Keams Canyon,
there were no Navajos. In 1904, they took in five
or six Navajo boys. There was animosity between the youth even there. They were always
raiding our childish possessions. Once you were
enrolled in a school, you continued there. My
grandfather came for me each spring and took
me back in the fall.*

Some of the older boys built rooms against
the overhanging ledges of the canyon walls near

the school. They laid up walls from the sandstone at hand. Here was their retreat from the routine of school life. They would let the little boys come if they would get wood for the fire. When Emory was one of the little boys he went out to get some wood. Coming back with an armful of sticks, he threw his firewood over the edge of the canyon wall. He was wearing some mittens that had been given him at the school Christmas party; a cord around his neck with a mitten on each end. A big stick of wood caught in the cord and Emory lost his balance and fell almost twenty feet down onto a ledge. He was knocked unconscious, and his collarbone was broken. A few hours later he was surprised to find himself in bed, in the daytime, in the infirmary. Dr. Breid, who took care of him, admired the plucky little boy and was good to him, and they became fast friends.

When Emory was thirteen, he was transferred to the Sherman Institute at Riverside, California, where he stayed for three years without going home. The boys would make themselves bows and arrows and go out hunting rabbits on Saturday. The school was away out in the desert then.

Students from the school furnished the manpower for the farmers around Riverside during the summer months. At first the oranges growing on trees seemed out of this world to the desert boys. There were big piles near the packing plants, available to the school kids, but they had to walk a long way to get them. They would lie around all day eating as many oranges as they could and then carry some back to stash away to eat later. Lazy boys would sometimes steal these oranges.

They worked picking strawberries for one cent per basket. You didn't eat too many if you wanted to make a dollar in a day. As a basket was filled it was left sitting in the row until a dozen were ready to be checked in. Each boy had to keep watch that the boy on the next row did not move the basket over onto his row.

According to Emory:

When I grew bigger I had a job driving a team, on a hay bailer, round and round all day, for which I was paid fifty cents. We also picked oranges on Saturday for hire, in season.

After three years in Riverside I was sent home to the Reservation. Now my mother had a third husband. I had been away so long that I didn't feel at home there, and I went to live in Bacabi with my cousin Susie, whose husband was my godfather. I did visit my mother and helped in whatever way that I could. I especially remember sleeping on the roof with my grandfather. He told me the story of how in his youth he had gone alone to Sante Fe, New Mexico. His young wife of a few months had been kidnapped by raiders, along with some children, and taken away and sold into slavery. Wickvaya went to the head man in Santa Fe and brought back not only Chosnysie but many other Hopi captives, on orders of the government — a saga in heroism in true Hopi style. I worked along with the men of the family in the cornfields and at the end of the summer I went to the Phoenix Indian School.

Food, Clothing, and Shelter

MY PEOPLE TOOK what was at hand and made
the best of it to provide the necessities of life,
and I was a participant and beneficiary during
my childhood, and while we lived for fifteen
years in Hotevilla, and later at the ranch. The
fertile soil in the valleys, small and large, that
drained water from their several watersheds,
made growing of crops possible. Water was obtained from the well, and fuel from the cedar
trees nearby. In places were to be found surface

deposits of coal. These resources, coupled with hard work, supported a population of a thousand souls for many years.

Hopis also farmed land at Moenkopi, about forty miles to the west from Oraibi as the crow flies. (The Hopi farmer took it on a jog trot.) There was rich valley land with water from big permanent springs, and a wash that drained a big watershed. A warmer climate, lower altitude, and longer growing season assured good crops every year, and provided Oraibi with an auxiliary corn basket.

At planting and harvest time the men would camp at Moenkopi for several days, but they always felt safer when they were atop the mesa at home in Oraibi. A few jaunts back to care for the growing crops during the summer were necessary; but at harvest time — what a hazard from Navajo raiders. After the Mormons colonized at Tuba City (about 1876), one mile from Moenkopi, Hopi families built homes at Moenkopi and lived there the year round.

Before the Spaniards came into our land, my people used only wild game for their meat — such as deer, antelope, and rabbit. From the Spaniards they learned to domesticate and use sheep and cattle for food, and the horse and donkey as beasts of burden. The first cattle that the Hopis had were found near Cedar Ridge (Highway 89), where a few head had strayed

from the herd as the Conquistadores passed
through, driving cattle with them for their meat
supply.

Corn was literally the "staff of life" in olden
days. The Hopis knew how to make their corn
grow in the sandy, arid soil. Farmers unfamil-
iar with the situation, who had to depend on the
corn they could raise, would surely starve. We
had our own native varieties — sweet corn, field
corn, blue corn, and yellow corn, red, white,
and mixed corn. One aimed to have on hand a
supply of corn, enough to last two years, so that
if there was a dry year, one's family wouldn't
starve. A desperate fear that it might not rain
and mature the corn was ever with us. No edible
thing was ever wasted. When I was a little girl
there were times when we went for weeks without having enough to eat. Then, when the early
corn was ripe, the whole family would move out
and camp at the cornfield and eat corn on the
cob three times a day and be glad to have it.

About two miles to the southeast of Oraibi,
off the mesa, there was a valley of rich, fertile
soil. The Oraibi Wash that ran through this valley drained a watershed extending some sixty
miles north into the Black Mountains. This land
was set aside for the use of the Chief and eight
or ten head men of the village. The Chief had
about ten acres nearest the wash, and the others

were alloted favorable areas, according to their rank.

When warm spring days started to melt the snow back in the mountains, the floodwaters could be seen approaching for miles. A watcher would give the word, and the town crier would give the order from his housetop: "Everybody report for work down in the valley." Men and women, boys and girls, even little children (I remember working there when I was no more than six years old), were required to respond to the call. Very old women and mothers of very young children remained in the village to care for the little ones and to prepare the food for the workers. The few men who were herding the sheep were also exempted. Everyone, taking whatever implements and baskets he had, ran to reach the wash ahead of the floodwaters. The Chief and the head men were there, each to direct the workers where to put dirt and brush in order to spread the water onto his land. First, the land of the Chief was well soaked. Then the water was turned onto the cornland of the next in rank, and then the next. This watering would assure the sprouting of the corn and make it "come up." Every man planted a small tract for early corn, but later was the time for the big planting, and again the whole village was ordered out to plant for the Chief and head men.

Again, when summer brought the hoped-and-prayed-for rains, the community responded to irrigate for their leaders. This time careful tending was necessary to guide the water to each hill of now growing corn. Hoeing and cultivating on these fields was also done by all the people.

When the landlord decided the corn was ready, a day was set and the workers gathered the long ears of ripened corn and piled them at the edge of the field nearest the village. The corn was then transported to the door of the owner on the mesa by a line of workers passing baskets and containers from hand to hand. There might be six or eight feet between the workers, but the line stretched from the field to the village. As a container was emptied it was passed back along the line. Now the Chief's corn was ready to dry and store.

There was time for the common man to care for his own cornland. This would be little areas anywhere that floodwaters would flow — sometimes on a hillside, sometimes in the bottom of a little wash. Clans had designated areas for their members. A man farmed a certain farm all his life, and his sons could enjoy the use of it, but it belonged to the clan and could not be disposed of. There was cooperative effort in planting and harvesting within the clan.

Fear of hunger was continuously in the

minds of men, and there were no lazy ones. All worked hard and prayed as well for a good harvest. The father led his family to the fields daily to make sure that no weed was allowed to rob the soil of any drop of moisture. Children hoed and threw rocks at rabbits, birds, and rodents. Scarecrows flapped their arms in the breeze, when there was a breeze. Shiny pieces of broken glass and tin were scattered about; the reflection of the sun on these bits had a discouraging effect on some of the pests.

After fighting these destroyers all summer, and when the kernels on the cob began to mature, then came the worst pest of all — great flocks of crows would fly in and settle down in a field. They devoured the corn in a hurry. Men took lunches and went out early, at sunup, to fight off the crows. Later the whole family came out to help; they shouted, threw rocks and sticks, and shot arrows or even a .22 gun to scare off the crows. The maturing corn must be saved.

Once a man went out to his cornfield, earlier than sunup. Lying in a depression, he covered himself with grass and weeds and waited. Pretty soon came one lone crow. He flew around the field a few times and then settled down at the edge of the field for a few minutes surveying the situation. Then he gave a few loud "caw caws," and here they came — it seemed like millions of crows — so many that Mr. Farmer could hardly decide in which direction to shoot his shotgun. But shoot he did, many times, killing many crows. He said that no crows came to bother his field for a long time.

When the corn was harvested and stored, it was a time of joyous thanksgiving. Years of bountiful harvest were happy years.

A prolonged period of dryness made the sad side of the picture. It was heartbreaking to come to the end of the month of August, after working hard all summer, hoping and praying for rain, watching in vain as the summer clouds arose from the horizon and sometimes gathering enough to promise rain, only to see them dissipate without dropping their moisture; seeing the corn, bean, melon, and squash plants stunted but still kept alive by the small bit of moisture retained in the soil, now beginning to wilt in the late, hot, summer sun — the prospect of a harvest vanishing — but still hoping. If only September would bring some good showers, and then if the frost would hold off until late October, as sometimes happens, the corn and beans would respond to the magic touch of water, and there could still be a harvest and corn in the storehouse. The prayer of the snake priests in their late August ceremony and dance implored, "Send us clouds, lightning, thunder, and rain.

Then will the corn mature, and there will be
food for the people. Then will there be joy in
the village; the children will play, the young
people will laugh, and all hearts will be filled
with thanksgiving." This fervent prayer came
from the heart. When these prayers were of no
avail, the people were faced with famine — no
hope for a crop for another year. There was no
laughter in the village. Hearts were filled with
dread of lingering hunger and starvation.

With modern communication and transportation, conditions have changed. Outside help
may now save villages from starvation — but
such was not the case one hundred years ago in
Oraibi. Sometimes families, or even whole villages, would migrate. The pueblo dwellers in
New Mexico, living along the valley of the Rio
Grande, nearly always had corn; and that was a
popular place to go. After taking stock of its supplies a family might decide to go now, while
there was food to last the 250-mile trip on foot,
or maybe there would be enough to last until
spring, then go in time to help plant corn. Once
the migrants reached their destination, they
would sell themselves into temporary slavery
for food. Often they would return to their own
village after the drought had passed. Sometimes
they never did return.

With hunger staring them in the face, families would dig into the ash piles and salvage every peach stone or kernel of corn; they would search the desert for whatever might be available — rabbits and other small animals, sweet-tasting cedar berries, wild greens, and small kernels from the heads of wild grasses. All the family would help in these projects. Wild potatoes, about as big as a marble, grew about. Men would go out gathering these and be gone as long as a week, maybe bringing back as much as fifty pounds in a burden basket. These little potatoes, when boiled and mashed with some real fine yellowish clay that gave them a buttery flavor, tasted good and were nourishing. (This clay was found several feet under ground near my home on the ranch. It is covered now, and no one knows exactly where it is.)

Sometimes food was denied the aged; babies fared poorly, and there were no fat people. Men would trade their silver and turquoise and beads for a few ears of corn. Every family was on its own. Even if a Chief had a lot of corn he would not share it. Some people would go and stand watching those who had corn, while they ate, hoping for a few kernels. I remember there were times when my mother ate very little so there would be more for her children. She watched us closely to keep us from going to the neighbors' houses while they were eating.

The story is told that one time only two families had corn left from the year before. It was piled neatly against the wall of the storeroom. One man bored a hole through the wall, a little hole that would not be noticed. He could reach in and get out one ear of corn at a time, but he was eventually found out.

It had been predicted that there would come a time when the Chief would so stray from the traditions of the past that the best corn land would be destroyed. This has literally come to pass. The rich land that once furnished the corn for the chief men of the village of Oraibi has now reverted to desert. (This came as a result of the schism in the village and the events of 1906, told in the chapter on "The Line.")

With the coming of spring 1907, there was no one to call out the villagers to work and no workers to respond to the call. Chief Tewaquap-tewa and Yokeoma and the others were in schools and prisons from California to New York, and the common men of the village also were scattered. The whole system of land use was broken up. The spring floods of 1907 ran uncontrolled for the first time. Erosion worked fast in the deep sandy soil. Before the men were returned, the channel of the Oraibi Wash was so deep that it was impossible to divert the water onto the land, and the cornland was lost forever. The wash now runs in a channel as deep as thirty feet in places, carrying the floodwaters swiftly away to the Little Colorado River.

After the corn was gathered and stored, then came the time for providing clothing for the family. A native variety of cotton grown principally at Moenkopi was the sole raw material for Hopi looms during the pre-Spanish era. When the Conquistadores came they brought with them herds of sheep, as well as the Catholic Fathers, who stayed on to carry out the saving of the souls of Hopis. The Spanish taught the Hopis that sheep would provide meat for food and fleece for their clothing. In due time, each family built up its own little flock of sheep, and wool gradually supplanted cotton. However, to this day, cotton is still kept on hand for use in weaving the traditional wedding robes.

The preparation of the raw cotton and the wool was carefully done by hand. All helped to pick the seeds from the cotton and to pull the burrs and little sticks out of the wool. Then the fleece was washed and beaten on the rocks as it dried. Then came the carding, spinning, and dying of the thread for both the warp and the woof. Ready-to-use cotton warp was used by some when the Trading Post made it available.

No woman ever sat at the Hopi looms. The men were expert weavers; they wove diligently all winter long in the various kivas. When one had enough to take care of his family's needs, he continued weaving to have a surplus on hand for trading. Hopi woven items were known far and wide, and people of other tribes came to barter for them.

A baby's first clothes were given by his paternal grandmother. These clothes maybe would consist of soft little pieces of used wool blankets for wrapping and swaddling. The baby was put on the cradleboard early. Fine cedar bark, softened between the hands until it became absorbent and sponge-like, was placed as a diaper to keep the cradleboard dry. If the cradleboard got wet it was put aside to dry. Fine clean sand was used to blot and absorb the moisture from the bark diapers, which were re-rubbed and the sand shaken off; the bark was put in the sun, and when completely dry it was rubbed between the hands again and was ready for use.

When a child was around two years of age, the maternal grandfather wove a special blanket, with different markings for a boy or girl. There was a black and white plaid pattern around the edge. This blanket was a passport into paradise. If the child died without having had this robe he could not enter there. The boy wore his robe around his shoulders shawl fashion, and the girl wrapped it around her body with the corners fastened at the right shoulder. When the child outgrew this small blanket, some other child could use it, but each child had to have his own newly made gift blanket.

In olden days, little Hopi boys wore no clothing until they were five or six years of age. In winter, they stayed inside to keep warm. If a boy went outside he wrapped himself in a blanket. The first garment a little boy wore was a kilt of a woven blanket some fifteen inches wide and long enough to go around his waist and lap a little. This kilt was a two-tone blue; blue background with darker blue circles six inches in diameter, centered one circle in the back and one in front. A cord was tied around the waist and the kilt folded over the cord to the inside, three or four inches. This was the basic garment for the boy and the grown man. In summer the upper part of the body was bare. In winter the man wrapped in a blanket. Moccasins made with rawhide soles and buckskin uppers served the men well for footwear. Woven leggings were worn for added warmth.

Levi's and western shirts are the Hopi man's favorite garb now. In the transition period from the kilt to Levi's, the men bought heavy unbleached muslin from the trading posts and sewed their own trousers and a shirt of figured cotton in their own ingenious pattern. Clothing was worn until it fell apart, and styles remained constant.

Women and girls dressed alike. A little girl was clothed earlier than her brother. The father wove her blanket-dress, dyed with native indigo to a dark blue, and sized to fit. For a woman it was about four by five and a half feet. It was folded crosswise and draped around the body over the right arm, leaving the left shoulder bare; the corners were fastened over the right shoulder. The open side was stitched together below the arm, forming a dress. A woven, red girdle four inches wide and two yards long ending in a long fringe was wrapped around the waist and then tucked under on the left side. A small blanket called a "back apron" was draped to cover the left shoulder and was tied under the right arm. When a woman was working inside the house she could dispense with the back apron, but she never went outside without it. In summer, women went barefoot. In winter, they wrapped their feet in sheepskins, with the wool inside and tied on with string.

When cotton yardage became available from the "traders," a length of gingham or calico was often used in the same manner as the back apron. Later, due to the influence of the government schools, the girls sewed cotton cloth into dresses. There are a few women, mostly living in Hotevilla, who still wear the traditional Hopi dress. Some buy dark cloth for the dress and use a bright piece for the back apron.

When I was a little girl, before I was old enough to go to school, I would sometimes wear my dress without the belt, because, being woven of wool, the clothing was so scratchy and itchy. There is one kachina who does not wear a belt. The tunic is just draped over the shoulder. More than once my young uncles made fun of me and fixed me up and called me that kachina and told me to go around the village singing the song of that certain kachina.

When I started going to the day school in Oraibi, we were given cotton union suits. Then as soon as I got home from school, my mother told me to take off the white man's clothes. I would sometimes leave on the cotton underwear because it felt good under that scratchy wool, but my mother would always discover it and make me take it off because of her deep scorn for the white man and his trappings.

The newly married Hopi couple usually went to live at the home of the bride's mother until such time as they could build a house of their own, the speed of which depended upon the pressure from within and the ambition of the young husband. The youngest daughter would likely stay and gradually take over the mother's household, and in a few years it would be the mother who would be living with her daughter in the latter's home.

Hopis build their houses close to each other to remind them that they are supposed to love each other. If one should build his house away from the others, they would say, "He is selfish. He does not love his neighbors." When a man decided to build a house he did not draw money from his bank account to pay for materials and labor. He gathered the materials provided by nature and drew from his reserve of good will (and that of his relatives) among his clan and friends, acquired from his own participation in such cooperative projects. The nearby sandstone cliffs invited the hammer and wedge to furnish rock for the walls. Logs for the beams that would support the roof could be obtained from nearby cedar trees if the room was not too large, but if the room was a big one, from the pines in the mountains sixty miles away. The materials for the roof were to be had from the trees and brush and earth at hand.

The house was built one room at a time, the existing wall of another house was used for one side, and thus only three walls had to be built. When a second room was added it often was built at the rear of the first; the third room would be built on top of the second, leaving the roof of the first room as a terrace porch.

The first step was to get out the sandstone. This the builder did by himself, working at cutting the blocks at odd times for as long as a year, depending upon how much time he had to devote to this task and how diligently he applied himself. When he had enough stone cut, he might kill a sheep from his own flock or buy one, and his wife and her family started cooking. The husband then invited his friends and neighbors to help transport the stone to the site of the proposed house. They formed a brigade and passed the building stone from hand to hand to the point where it was to be laid into the walls. This part of the project was usually completed in one day, with dinner served at noon to all the workers. It was sometimes several weeks later before the walls were erected.

Whenever the community came to help they had to be fed. After each operation, the builder sometimes needed time in which to acquire the necessary food. It was easier to feed the women when they worked; they would settle for corn and beans, while the men would want meat and something better.

The women made the mortar and sometimes helped lay the walls; even sometimes it was all women working. As many as could find room to work helped lay up the stone. To make the mortar, first they dug a hole about a foot deep and three feet in diameter near the new house. Sand

and clay were carried and piled near this hole.
If there was a puddle of rain-water nearby everyone carried water in her jug. If there was no
rainwater, they carried the water from the well;
everyone had her jug full, so there was a lot of
water on hand before they started mixing. Water
and clay were put into the hole and let soak a
while. Then sand was added, and the women sat
around the hole and mixed the mortar with their
hands, until it was satiny and smooth, when
they lifted it out and piled it nearby. This process was repeated until there was a big pile of
mortar. (The men make mortar now with hoes,
but it is not as good.) Next the women formed
a line and passed the mortar in double hands
full to the men working at the walls. This clay
and sand set hard like cement.

After the walls were laid, the beams for the
flat roof were put in place about three feet apart.
Next, little cedar logs about two inches in diameter, gathered and ready, were laid at right
angles to the beams, three to four inches apart.

Now, there must be more mortar for the
roof. While the women made the mortar, the
men gathered fresh, green rabbit brush and arms
full of bee plant, which they carried in bundles
on their backs to the house being born. A six-
inch layer of green brush was carefully packed
at right angles to the little logs, and over the
brush was spread a six-inch layer of mortar,

again passed from hand to hand and up the ladder to the roof, in double hands full. Men were ready on the roof to take the mortar and carefully place it over the brush and tamp it down; lastly, three inches of dry clay well tamped by the feet finished the fine waterproof roof. Days later, the women made more mortar and with it smoothly plastered the inside walls; they then put a thick layer on the floor and smoothed it down, which when hardened made a good hard floor. So, after many weeks and the labor of many hands and many meals served, the house was ready for occupancy.

Barter and Trade

THERE WAS ALWAYS an exchange of wares and
goods among the individuals in a village. Occasionally there would be a big swap day when
a woman brought whatever she had in surplus,
or cooked her specialty and brought it to the
plaza, to trade with her neighbors; they traded
corn, beans, piki, blue cornmeal, and peaches.
On any day, a housewife, when she was getting
ready to cook, might find she was short on an
item, and she would pick up something that she

had plenty of and go out into the plaza, where at her request the town crier would announce, "You women who are in your homes, there is a swap here in the plaza. Come and see it. Come with gladness in your hearts."

My three-year-old brother Henry was a skinny little kid and a fussy eater. He didn't like the bread made from wheat flour. One day mother made a big stack of wheat tortillas, which she set on the table at noon. Henry cried and said he wouldn't eat any of that. Mother picked up the basket of tortillas, went to the plaza, where the crier called out notice of a trade. One of the first women to respond traded for piki, and Henry ate heartily.

When his supplies of corn and beans were getting low, my father would take a blanket one hundred miles to Winslow, where he would trade it for ten dollars worth of flour, sugar, and salt, which he brought back on his donkey. Flour was cheap, and he got all the donkey could carry in twenty-five-pound sacks. Father kept his loom humming so that he would be able to keep his family from starving.

After the harvest was over men would go to the neighboring Hopi villages, going from kiva to kiva to exchange wares. During the spring there was always traffic in commodities between tribes within a reasonable radius. Trade extended far, as shown by the seashells and coral found in Hopi jewelry. This was a two-way deal with trading parties of two or more men, even as many as ten, taking their goods on the backs of their donkeys and going on a venture. Oraibi, because of its geography, was at the crossroads. Traders came from Utah, Hualapai, Zuni, and from New Mexico pueblos — even as far as Taos — to barter and trade for Hopi textiles and produce.

Hopi traders went to Winslow and all the little towns along the Santa Fe railroad, as far as Flagstaff. They traversed the country in safety, as most of the tribes were friendly. They often went by Prescott to gather cowhides that were to be found on the outskirts of that town. If they were lucky they found many. These they cut in wide strips and rolled into bundles and tied to the burro pack, later to be tanned and used for soles in the making of moccasins. They collected every kind of container they could find about the towns. A five-gallon can was a big prize. These made a pleasant tinkling sound as the donkey plodded along, which heralded the approach of the homecoming traders. These small articles were used as homecoming gifts and were treasured and used for carrying and storing both water and food.

The Zunis found formations of turquoise in their area, which they gathered and used for their chief medium of exchange. Their traders came on foot, two or more, carrying their merchandise in little bundles. If he was lucky, the Zuni trader would catch a ride part of the way with a Hopi freight outfit coming in from Holbrook.

Burros ran wild in herds in New Mexico. Men would round up a herd of burros and drive them to a Hopi village, taking a week or ten days to make the trip. At Oraibi, they would hold the burros in a sort of natural cove overnight. In the morning the Hopi men went out to barter. The boys of the village always followed the men out to watch. The trade was one manta for one burro. Each man selected the donkey he wished to acquire. It was up to the buyer to get a rope on his animal, separate it from the herd, and get it home. This is where the sport came in, as the individual raced along after his "buy," trying to steer the untamed creature toward the village. Men and beasts would be running in all directions, which furnished many a laugh to the youngsters.

The donkey is fairly easy to tame and train to carry a rider or a pack of green corn shocks, dried corn on the cob, melons, vegetables, or wood. The Hopi prized this patient beast of burden, for it lightened his load considerably; each family possessed one or more burros, according to his wealth.

Utes came on horseback from the North bringing beautiful white buckskins, prized by

the Hopis for making moccasins for their brides
— also men's moccasins, dyed a beautiful brown.
As the Ute trader neared the village he might
gather a bundle of wood to trade. Hualapais also
traded buckskins mostly.

The Hopi men took over the business of trading with the other tribes and conducted it in an
orderly and business-like manner. But when the
Navajo trader came, that was something else
again. He came when the weather had cooled
off in the fall. Often his wife came with him. In
his wagon he brought several carcasses of mutton, sometimes as many as a dozen, if he were
that rich. He also brought piñon nuts, a luxury
item in great demand. He might have one hundred pounds of these bean-sized nuts from the
piñon trees, in gunny sacks. He was loaded. As
he drove his wagon into the village, Mr. Navajo
was invited by someone to be his overnight guest.
The trading could be done in the morning, and
the Navajo family would be homeward bound in
the afternoon.

When the Navajo was ready to trade, the
Hopi women ran out and lifted the wagon cover
to see what he had; each took hold of a piece of
meat that she wanted, and the bargaining began.
Neither the Navajo nor the Hopi knew many
words of the other's language, just the names of
the items, and there was much pantomime and
charades and sign language mixed with Hopi
and Navajo — and a little English maybe. Mr.

Navajo would begin by making it known that, "For this hind quarter I want dried peaches."

Mrs. Hopi brought out her peaches, and the amount would be settled — maybe two baskets or three baskets full of dried peaches for a hind quarter of mutton. Perhaps Mrs. Navajo might think she was being shortchanged, so Mrs. Hopi would finally add another handful of peaches for good measure. As Mrs. Navajo gave her assent, Mrs. Hopi took the meat to her house, and the next in line took up the bargaining. Mr. Navajo would name what he wanted in exchange for each piece of meat: "I want green corn, two baskets full, for this piece," or, "I want piki for this." Mrs. Hopi might say, "I have no piki. Will you take beans or melons?" "No, I want piki." Some woman who happened to have a supply of piki would bring it out and take the meat, and so it continued until the meat was all gone.

Now, Mr. Navajo opened his sack of piñons, and the bargaining really waxed hot. He loved the dried peaches and Mrs. Hopi wanted the piñon nuts. The younger women would stand in the doorways, and the men loitered about as they enjoyed the drama.

The Hopi women would bring out their peaches in small baskets and form a line, each in turn trading a basket full of peaches for a basket half full of piñons, taking them home and coming back for more. Maybe a woman had no peaches and she would bring corn or piki. As she moved up and offered her basket, Mr. Navajo would say, "No, I don't want that. I want peaches." "Mrs. Hopi would say, "This is as good as peaches." Poor woman. Sometimes he would say, "All right this time, but don't bring any more. I want peaches." Or a friend might let her have a basket of peaches to trade for piñons; then Mrs. Hopi would say, "I will do something for you for this — make piki or something." The line kept moving and the trading continued until the wagon load was finally exchanged; when Mr. Navajo would hitch up his horses and drive slowly out of the village, heading homeward, and everyone was pleased to have variety in the larder.

The advent of the trading post in the 1870's changed the pattern of merchandising, but it was bartering and trading. The trader was also a stockman, and his flock of sheep increased daily as he took in sheep in exchange for goods — on the hoof, a carcass, the sheared wool, and even the pelt. Food products and products of the loom and jewelry were included in trade. Later, as cattle replaced sheep, more or less, they were traded too. The trader expected to buy the bulk of the cattle in the fall, when they were in good shape after summer grazing.

One year the trader was offering twelve dollars a head for steers. The government stockmen from Keams Canyon suggested to Emory that they sell direct to the buyer and bypass the trader, advising they could realize more money that way. Emory persuaded several men to follow this advice. They gathered their steers and had them ready to drive to Winslow. Emory met the trader who said, "Why don't you sell your cattle to me?" Emory replied, "We think we can make more money this way." The trader got mad and red in the face as they talked and shouted and even screamed, "I can't make any money if you don't sell me your cattle."

By the time Emory had finished his business and returned to the camp where the men were watching the herd, the trader had been there before him and convinced the men that they could not carry out their plan and would lose out by doing so. Emory sat until late in the night arguing, "Let us try it and see. It won't hurt to try it out this one time." He finally prevailed, and they drove the cattle on to Winslow. Emory went ahead with the government agent who went all the way to see the project through. They ordered cattle cars to be waiting on the siding when the herd got there, and there was no delay in loading. Emory and the government stockmen rode the cattle train to Los Angeles where they sold the livestock, realizing four times as much as they would have, had they sold in Oraibi to the trader. Needless to say, we still do not sell the cattle to the trader.

The Line

EVEN THOUGH I WAS only seven years old at the time, I remember most vividly the happenings of September 6 and 7, 1906. Those days brought to a climax events going back more than fifteen years, and they had a profound effect on my life, as well as the lives of each and every inhabitant of the village of Old Oraibi.

In the year 1890, Lololama, Chief of Oraibi, along with chiefs from four other villages, went on a government-sponsored trip to Washington,

D.C., seeking good will and better understanding. Lololama returned convinced by what he had seen and heard that his people would benefit by embracing some of the changes offered by the government. He spoke out boldly, urging his people to move down off the mesa where they would be nearer their farms and their water supply and to send their children to school.

To the Hostiles, this was heresy. Ancient shrines could not be moved or forsaken. The good Hopi traditions had guided them to a good life; why should they be abandoned? Sending children to school was not the Hopi way of education. They had on-the-job training. Children learned to care for the sheep and raise corn in the day-by-day school of experience. Girls learned from their mothers to grind corn, prepare the food, and care for the household. Men and boys met in the kiva in winter time for lessons in history, religion, and traditions — all taught in story and song. Here also was learned respect for their elders and for tribal and clan codes.

Lololama's right-hand man at this time was Yokeoma, who stood firmly for following the old traditions. As Lololama had said in Washington, his people were blind and deaf to any change in their ways. In due time Yokeoma parted ways with Lololama with a following of more than half the village. Yokeoma was in his 50's and was referred to as the "Aged Chief." Now there were two chiefs in one village; Lololama of the Friendlies and Yokeoma of the Hostiles — a house divided. From this time on there was increasing contention over the attitude toward the influence of the white man.

Upon the death of Lololama in 1900, Tewaquaptewa, a man about thirty years of age, became Chief of the Friendlies.

A few years before, there had been an epidemic of smallpox among the Hopis. The Department of Public Health had ordered general vaccination and fumigation of all houses. The agency superintendent accompanied by some Indian police went with the health officers to carry out this order. At Shungopovi, they encountered active resistance from an aggressive Hostile group, which successfully defied them and put them out of the village. Reinforcements had to be summoned to accomplish the vaccination and fumigation order. This situation was unbearable to the Friendlies of Shungopovi, and taking matters into their own hands they forced several of the most difficult Hostile families out of the village.

The exiles went over to Oraibi where they were welcomed and taken in by the Oraibi Hostiles. Yokeoma had previously sought support from the Hostiles in Shungopovi in resisting the health officers in Oraibi in this same matter. The presence of the Shungopovi Hostiles in Oraibi aggravated the already tense situation, increasing the ever-widening schism to the point of invading the ceremonials. All during the summer of 1906, instead of being a community project, ceremonials would be sponsored by one faction or the other. If the Hostiles were performing, the Friendly women would shut their doors and stay inside all day while their men folk spent the day hoeing corn in the fields. If the Friendlies were the sponsors, the Hostiles refused to be spectators. In all this, the Shungopovis were a most disturbing factor.

The Home Dance comes in July. It marks the time when the kachinas return to their legendary home in the San Francisco Peaks, there to stay until the end of the harvest season. The Home Dancers, dressed in their kachina regalia, enter the plaza and perform their ritual eight times during the day, beginning early in the morning and ending late in the afternoon. Between each song and dance they retire to a resting place outside the village and out of view of the plaza.

This dance was being sponsored by the Hostiles in 1906. The men dancers were leaving the plaza after their final appearance, going toward the age-old trail to the sacred kiva, where it was the custom to remove their costumes and masks and ceremoniously seal and store them until the opening of the next ceremonial year. As the kachinas came to a narrow passage, where two houses were only ten feet apart, they found their way blocked by strong men of the Friendlies who had stationed themselves strategically and stepped out quickly forming a line shoulder to shoulder, barring the way and preventing the kachinas from going through.

It was beneath the dignity of the kachinas to physically contest this challenge. They argued for about an hour, rehearsing the traditional respect due them, to no avail. In humiliation the kachinas turned back and retired from the plaza to the resting place and there disrobed. This was a deliberate insult on the part of the Friendlies, with all eyes upon them. The tension built up to fever heat, until by the end of the summer there were threats of driving the Hostiles out of the village.

Frequently reiterated during this time was a prophecy that there would come a time when the village would be divided and one of the groups would be driven off the mesa forever and that the decision of who should go and who should stay was to hinge upon the ability of one party to push the other over a line which should be drawn on the ground.

Chief Tewaquaptewa went to Keams Canyon, protesting to the Superintendent (Lemmon) that the Hostiles from Shungopovi were going to build houses in Oraibi, although they were not wanted and there was neither water nor cornland sufficient for the people already there. He said that if they attempted to build houses, the walls would be torn down as fast as they were put up; also that the time for the initiation ceremony was drawing near, and he didn't want the Shungopovis in Oraibi at that time; they would not be permitted at the initiation. They had to go, and at once. Moreover, Tewaquaptewa was outraged because the Shungopovi priests had usurped the authority of the Oraibi priests to consecrate cornmeal for ceremonial use. Superintendent Lemmon advised Tewaquaptewa to be patient, and the Hostiles would be pressed to make the first overt move.

The Commissioner of Indian Affairs visited Oraibi sometime during the summer of 1906 to try to settle the dispute between the Hostiles and the Friendlies, which seemed to be getting out of hand. His report to the Department of Interior shows that he had an unsatisfactory conversation with Yokeoma, Hostile Chief, and that he held a council on the mesa in the open air on a moonless night in the plaza of the pueblo.

He discussed the matter with Tewaquaptewa as follows:

"Descending the trail I noticed that I was 'shadowed' by three men, evidently Indians, who kept out of my way as long as anyone else

was within speaking distance, but as soon as I was alone, drew nearer. As I entered my room, which was a little ell of the principal cottage at the foot of the mesa, the three men pushed in after me, and on striking a light I found my visitors to be the Friendly chief and two of his supporters. One of the two volunteered to act as interpreter and informed me that the chief wished to ask me a few questions when no white man and no Hostiles were within hearing. The first was, where had I come from? I answered that I was from Washington. What was my position? Commissioner of Indian Affairs, in charge of the people of his race all over the country. For what purpose had I come to Oraibi? To see with my own eyes the condition of the Oraibi Indians — how they were living, how white employees of the government were taking care of them, and so on. How long was I going to stay? I should leave probably the next day. Had I come to settle the quarrel between the Hostiles and the Friendlies? No, for that would take a longer time than I could spare then; and moreover, I had been in hope that, like white people who had differences, they would get together, talk things over, and settle their troubles among themselves, instead of falling back, like so many little children, upon the government. When was I going to remove the Hostiles from Oraibi, send them away to some distant place to live, and divide their land and other property among the Friendlies? I was not contemplating ever doing this. They knew better, for Superintendent Lemmon had told them this was what I was going to do; and now, how soon was I going to start the business? I thought they were mistaken; they had misunderstood Mr. Lemmon, . . . No, indeed; they had not misunderstood Mr. Lemmon; he knew what Washington was going to do, and he had told them again and again. If I didn't know it, that showed that I didn't know what Washington was about; so why did I say that I was from Washington, and had charge of the Indians, when I was ignorant of this program? . . .

"His heart was set on the question of how to get rid of the Hostiles, and he soon took his leave with a rather discouraged air.

"Before I left the neighborhood, and after considerable discussion of the situation with the most intelligent white persons thereabout, I reached the conclusion that, much as such a resort is always to be deplored, I should probably have nothing left for me this season but to make a demonstration with troops which would convince the ring leaders of the Hostile faction that they could gain nothing by further hostility." (Report to Secretary of Interior, 1906, pages 118–125.)

The crisis was precipitated prematurely during the first week of September, 1906, when the two factions came to an actual physical struggle. Tewaquaptewa, whose following was slightly outnumbered by the Hostiles, received private information of a plot to assassinate him; indeed he understood that the Shungopovis, rather than the Oraibians, were the instigators of the plot. Tewaquaptewa called his council together that night at his house on the northern edge of the village, September 6, and they spent the night preparing for an attack on the Hostiles in the morning. During the night he sent word to Yokeoma and his followers, who were also in council, that the Shungopovis would have to leave at once and that anyone taking their part must leave with them. No reply was made. Near daybreak Tewaquaptewa sent another messenger asking if the Hostiles intended to leave peaceably. To this, Yokeoma gave no answer.

On Friday, September 7, 1906, at about 6:30 a.m., Buhunimptewa, as assistant snake priest and Hostile belonging in Oraibi, went to the Mennonite Mission, two miles down off the mesa, telling the Reverend Epp that serious trouble was brewing between the two factions. After a hasty breakfast, Reverend Epp, accompanied by Mrs. Gertrude Gates, an interested observer of Hopi culture, who appears to have been staying at the mission at this time, and Ed Gannett of the mission, drove to the school cottage in Mrs. Gates' wagon. There they informed Miss Elizabeth Stanley, school principal, and Miss Miltona Keith, the field nurse, of the state of affairs in Oraibi. Miss Stanley rode in the wagon, but Miss Keith rode on her pony, and they hurried to the village. On the way they met a man named Phillip, who was running to summon his father, who was working at the mission; he said that all men who had gone out early to work in the fields or to tend sheep were needed in the village because their families were in danger of being evicted from their homes. The party arrived at Tewaquaptewa's house around 8:00 a.m., where they found a score or more Friendlies clustered around their Chief, outside the house. The group was frequently augmented by two's and three's. There were no guns to be seen, but the men had a determined air.

Miss Stanley, representing Washington, spoke to Tewaquaptewa, with Fred Jenkins and later Lahpoo, brother of the Chief, acting as interpreters. Miss Stanley said that she had heard of Tewaquaptewa's plan to drive the Hostiles out that morning, suggesting that when Mr. Leupp (the Commissioner) told the Hopis at Oraibi to settle this difficulty among themselves, she thought he meant them to do by council and not by fighting. She advised them to leave their arms at home so as not to involve themselves and others in serious consequences.

Miss Keith spoke much in the same vein,

adding that if Tewaquaptewa or any of his men injured anyone they might be arrested and punished. Tewaquaptewa and others speaking simultaneously, avowed their indifference to the possibility of soldiers being sent to punish them, saying, "Let them come. We want them to come." Any arms they might have in their possession were for self-defense: "We are afraid the Hostiles will shoot us." Miss Stanley tried to persuade Tewaquaptewa to lay aside his arms; he would agree only on the condition that the Hostiles would do the same. She then requested him to remain where he was and to keep his men with him until she and the others had held a conference with the Hostiles. Lahpoo interpreting said, "They will be here." The Reverend Epp also urged the young chief to reconsider and to act carefuly and wisely. As the group turned to seek conference with the Hostiles, the Friendlies called to them to take the same interpreters, to say neither more or less than had been said to them, and to hurry, as they wished to get the business over with as soon as possible.

Within ten minutes, the mediators were assembled with Yokeoma and his men seated in a circle in a room of one of the Hostile houses; there were about fifty men, including the Shungopovis. They declined to come out and talk, so the mediators went inside the house. Miss Stanley and Miss Keith spoke again, being especially

careful to say only what they had said to the
other faction, using the same interpreters. The
Reverend Epp, who spoke Hopi, listened to
ensure honest interpretation. Miss Stanley was
just at the point of asking them to promise not
to use arms if they had any, when the doorway
was suddenly filled with men crowding rapidly
into the room, led by Chief Tewaquaptewa. The
Friendlies asked the white people to leave at
once, saying they had been too long already; the
interpreters called loudly and pushed the white
mediators out of the doorway. Quoting Miss
Stanley, "The melee was beginning when I, the
last *pahana* going out, found myself jostled into
the plaza. The streets entering the plaza seemed
full of excited Hopis running toward the house
we had just left, and I heard Ed Gannett advising me, 'Better get out of here; there's going to
be a scrap.'"

Tewaquaptewa loudly ordered the Shungopovis to leave the village at once, whereupon
Yokeoma said they should not leave and that his
(Oraibi) people would stand by them. Tewaquaptewa answered, "You will go too, then."

Thereupon, the Friendlies set about clear-
ing the village of Shungopovis. They began at
the very spot where they stood; but every
Friendly who laid hold of a Shungopovi to put
him out of doors was attacked from behind by
an Oraibi Hostile, so that the three went wres-

tling and struggling out of the door together. There was great commotion as the Friendlies carried out the Hostiles, pushing and pulling, the Hostiles resisting, struggling, kicking, and pulling the hair of their adversaries. The Hostiles were taken bodily, one by one to the northern outskirts of the village, and put down on the far side of a line which had been scratched in the sandstone, parallel to the village, some time before.

After evicting the Hostile men, the Friendlies went into each home and forcibly ejected each family, driving them out to join their menfolk on the other side of The Line. A struggling stream of humanity — men, women, and children — poured out of their houses past Tewaquaptewa's house and out of the village, being shoved and dragged and pulled by Tewaquaptewa and his excited followers. Those resisting had their clothing torn and were bruised and scratched; the majority went passively, carrying burdens, the men with set faces and the women and children frightened and crying. Tewaquaptewa's lieutenants ran rapidly back and forth between the village and the open, escorting and driving out individuals and families, hurrying all along, excitedly calling commands to the ejected and to one another; they looked wild-eyed and exhibited real fanaticism, for this event was the result of deep traditions, both factions claiming it had to be; their fathers had predicted it, saying, "The Hopis have always done this way now and then. Two chiefs cannot rule in the same village. One must go."

My father, knowing that trouble was brewing, had told the boy who took his sheep out that day to drive them toward the Hotevilla spring that night. He spent the night in the Hostile council. My mother, hearing the rumor that we might be expelled from the village, had made ready some food, a jug of water, and blankets.

There was an underground little room in our house, our secret hiding place in case of war or trouble. The entrance was a hole in the floor, covered with a sheepskin on which my mother sat as she ground her corn. There was a little window to the outside for light and air. On this morning mother put her children into this hiding place — my married sister, Verlie, about sixteen; my brother Rincon, twelve; myself, seven; and my brother Henry, two. She watched and kept telling us what was happening, saying, "Don't be afraid. Nothing will happen to you." After a while she lifted the sheepskin and said for us to come on out. She started helping us up, as the sides were steep. Just at that moment, in came Tewaquaptewa's men, who started jerking us out. I was so little, I can't remember it all. One of the men said, "The time has come for you to go, so come on out of your hiding place."

Then another man, I remember him because his neck was crooked and he was more fierce and began pushing us, and as he shoved me I fell and rolled down the steps. As we left the house, my mother handed each of us a bundle of food or clothing to carry. We walked into the plaza and were driven out of the village with the others. Many of the Friendly women sat on the flat housetops clapping their hands and yelling at us, making fun of us as we walked away from our home and village.

One man, a Hostile, had been roasting his corn the day before, green corn in the husks put into a preheated pit, covered with earth, and left all night. The corn is dried, and when it is boiled later, it tastes like fresh green corn. This man had gone early in the morning to bring his corn home. When he got back to the village with his several burros loaded with this baked corn, we had been driven out. They wouldn't let him go to his house, so he drove the burros out where the Hostiles were gathered and unloaded the corn on the big flat sandstones, and that is what we ate that day.

After the village was cleared of Hostiles, there were several hours of inactivity. To me and the other children it was like a picnic, as we played around on the rocks, unaware of the tragedy that was being enacted. From 10:00 a.m. to about 3:00 p.m. the Hostiles held

together, sitting on the hot rocks in the sun, and
the Friendlies stood around in groups, guarding
them and at intervals charging on them in a
fruitless endeavor to dislodge and drive them
away from the village. No weapons were used.
The Friendlies simply tried to force the Hostiles onward by physical strength, pushing and
pulling, scolding and insulting, yelling mostly,
"Drive the fellows out." Then there would be a
period of discussion of the old traditions. The
Hostiles said they knew that some one had to
go, it was according to prediction; but each faction maintained that it should be the others to
leave.

The Friendlies were slightly outnumbered,
but they made up for it in increased enthusiasm.
A few from both factions were out herding or
working in the fields, having gone out early in
the day.

As the day waned, Tewaquaptewa lost some
of his fiery spirit and seemed to listen more atten-
tively, even anxiously, to the timely word of
the white people present. He acquiesced to a
proposition to let Miss Stanley, Miss Keith, and
the Reverend Epp and Mrs. Gates go to the
Hostiles for the purpose of arbitration. The
whites approached the Hostile group, calling out
to Yokeoma, who came out with his character-
istic dignity and listened courteously to what

was said. When asked if they were all provided with necessities, Yokeoma answered that it was the Friendlies who should be ousted. They were the ones who had departed from the traditions. The Hostiles did not wish to obtain food; they wanted to go back to their homes in the village.

After the council with Yokeoma, some of the Friendlies asked the whites what to do about the sheep and other belongings of the Hostiles. They were told that all property of every description was still the property of the Hostiles. It was further decided that two interpreters, Tewaquaptewa, a man from Moenkopi, and the people representing Washington should meet with four Hostile leaders, where an ultimatum would be delivered by Tewaquaptewa, as follows:

The Hostiles should move on to the Hotevilla spring and remain there only until Washington could be heard from. The Friendlies wished them to move farther away.

The Hostiles should be allowed to come into the village to get their belongings, three men at a time, without molestation or mistreatment from the Friendlies. Tewaquaptewa announced there would be no stealing, and he set a guard to see to it. The Hostiles came and went for some time, bringing bedding and provisions.

Miss Keith, riding about on her pony, kept an eye on developments. She sent a messenger to Mr. Lemmon at Keams Canyon, apprising him of the situation. He arrived at Oraibi late in the evening.

Around four o'clock Yokeoma finally yielded to the continued pressure from the Friendlies. He stood up, and with all eyes on him, took a sharp rock in his hand and drew a line on the sandrock. Taking his stand with his back to the line he said, "Well, it will have to be this way now. If you pass me over this line, then I will walk." (He meant that he and his people would leave.)

Tewaquaptewa immediately jumped to the challenge. The two chiefs faced each other, each with his hands on the shoulders of his opponent. Their men rushed into the conflict, each eager to add his weight and exert his strength. Yokeoma was tall and thin. He was pushed up above the heads of the mass, gasping for breath; then he disappeared, and eventually he was passed over the line. A shout went up as Yokeoma, badly disheveled and trampled, was helped to his feet, and his men made sure that he was not hurt. As soon as he could collect himself, Yokeoma left the knot of men around him and started walking the trail to the Hotevilla spring. We all gathered our bundles and followed him.

It was dark when we got to the spring, but soon there were forty or fifty campfires burning, and preparations for sleeping under the trees

were under way. A few days later it rained, and
the weather turned colder. A shelter of brush and
trees was thrown up, reinforced with blankets,
shawls, gunny sacks, and pieces of old canvas,
anything for protection against the cold. The
dreary picture of the women and children
crouching under this crude shelter persuaded
Tewaquaptewa to further leniency. He gave
four more days in which the Hostiles might go
into the village, in groups of three, and bring out
their belongings. Many Hostiles expressed
themselves: "We don't want to go back to the
village and get our food. We want to go back
to our homes and live there as we have always
done."

Superintendent Lemmon said to Yokeoma,
"I am sorry that you are going away. I want you
here for my friend." Yokeoma replied, "I do not
want to go away from here." And the misery in
the old man's face testified that the words came
from his heart.

Days dragged, each augmenting the misery
of the exiles in their improvised shelters; the cold
increased, and each day decreased the hope of
going back to their comfortable houses in Oraibi.
The need of better shelter was urgent. There
was neither time nor manpower to quarry sandstone and gather the other materials to build
proper Hopi houses. The men went to work with
axes chopping cedars and preparing to build

hogans like those of the Navajos — poles standing upright, leaning to the center, and cracks
filled with mud. In a few weeks with all hands
helping there were forty to fifty hogans ready
for use.

We were not accustomed to the Navajo way
of cooking and heating with an open fire in the
middle of the floor and the smoke going out of a
hole in the center of the roof. Nearly every day
a house or something in it would catch fire.
Everyone kept a container with water on hand,
and when the alarm was given everyone ran to
help. Even *I* remember grabbing my little bottle
of water and running to help put out fires. The
hogans were pretty well finished before "they"
took the men away.

It had been understood that the Mesa Verde
area in Colorado was to be our destination. Some
of the clans claimed to have originated there.
But after about a week, Yokeoma stood by the
spring one morning, looked out over the valley,
and said, "I am staying here. Anyone who wants
to, can go on." None were anxious, and none
did go on.

While we were camping under the trees,
the word went out that "they" were coming to
take us away and kill us. Then my mother and
other women hid their jewelry. I was with my
mother as she gathered her strings of turquoise
and other jewelry and tied them with a cloth into

a bundle as big as a cantaloupe. I went out with her to a cedar tree under which she dug a hole about eighteen inches deep. She put a flat rock in the bottom of the hole, then the jewelry, then another rock, then she filled the hole with dirt; if she was killed no one would get her jewelry; if she lived she would go and get it back again.*

There are many big flat sandstones cropping out of the ground on the outskirts of Old Oraibi. One of them marks The Line. An inscription was scratched there by a young man named Robert Selena. Robert was a student at the Indian School at Keams Canyon and was home in the summer of 1906. He took it upon himself to mark the spot:

WELL IT HAVE TO BE DONE

THIS WAY NOW

THAT WHEN YOU PASS ME OVER THIS LINE

IT WILL BE DONE   SEPT. 8, 1906

---

* Years later my father got sick and mother paid the medicine man with pieces of her jewelry. Father was sick for a long time, and I know now that the medicine man could not cure him because he had a nervous breakdown; but before he got well, the medicine man had most of mother's jewelry. My father bought the jewelry back, piece by piece as he could, and gave it back to his wife, because it belonged to her family. My older sister had it until her death. Now, my brothers have it in their keeping. It is supposed to be for all the family to use at dances and ceremonials.

AUTHOR'S NOTE

The important and interesting event in Hopi history covered in the preceding chapter has been often referred to, but the facts have been sketchy and garbled. Information given by Helen Sekaquaptewa and her husband and others who were there has been supplemented and augmented and verified by the author from records in the Indian Section of the National Archives in Washington, D.C.

Soon after September 7, 1906, the Indian Commissioner requested that government employees, teachers, missionaries, and other observers write their own accounts of the affair in detail. Original letters dated not more than two weeks later form a voluminous file (#75) in the National Archives; the writers include the Reverend J. P. Epp of the Mennonite mission; Mrs. Gertrude Gates, an interested observer of Hopi culture who spent months camping outside Oraibi but was apparently staying at the mission at this time; Ed Gannett of the mission; Miss Elizabeth Stanley, in charge of the schools at Oraibi; and Miss Miltona Keith, field matron. These writers give a lively description of the happenings.

Another source of information is *The Annual Report of the Commissioner of Indian Affairs to the Secretary of the Interior* for the year 1906.

The Aftermath

Entry of Superintendent Lemmon, October 25, 1906:

I talked to Yokeoma. He desires his people returned to their village; Tewaquaptewa to be beheaded, which he says will end all the trouble.

The next day I took Tewaquaptewa with me to talk to Yokeoma. The latter firmly stood his ground and stoutly maintained that tradition required that the Chief who had departed from the Hopi way should have his head cut off, and

[85]

*again requested that Tewaquaptewa be be-
headed.*

On November 8, 1906, the superintendent
was back at Hotevilla with soldiers. He called
the men together and again urged the benefits
of complying with the government orders and
sending the children to school. A few men did
promise to cooperate, among them my sister
Verlie's young husband. These were permitted
to stay with their families. But the others
demanded that the white people go away so that
the Hopi children would not be ruined by learning of their civilization; they vowed that they
would not change their ways. Whereupon seventy-five men were placed under arrest and
taken to Keams Canyon by the troops, where
they were sentenced to ninety days of hard labor
and longer if they remained obstinate.

*Entry of Superintendent Lemmon, Novem-
ber 8, 1906:*
*The organization of the police has been com-
pleted, and the time the prisoners will serve will
begin today. We have ordered four tents to
shelter the men. Three for the men and one for
the foreman.*

February 18, 1907:
*The ninety days are up and many would not
promise to obey. Five finally did, after much per-*

suasion, and were sent home, which only made
the others more stubborn. After a few more
weeks the rest were sent home in time to help
with the spring planting and the building of
houses.

Some dozen or more men in their early 30's,
considered potential leaders, even men with families, were sent to the Indian School in Carlisle,
Pennsylvania, for five years. (Emory's father
was one of these.) Carlisle barracks is the oldest
continuously used army post and goes back to
days of the Revolutionary War. Some of the barracks were built by Hessian prisoners of war.
In the late 1880's it was converted into a school
for Indians from all over the nation. Jim Thorpe
went here. It is no longer used as a school for
Indians but is a college for U.S. Army officers
training.

Some of the older men, including my father,
who were considered responsible for the affairs
of the village, were given a punitive sentence of
a year in prison at Fort Huachuca in southern
Arizona. Yokeoma and Twashongniwa, leader
of the Shungopovites, were deposed and sent to
Fort Huachuca and were to be exiled from the
Hopi reservation forever.

The records show that Yokeoma was
released from Fort Huachuca along with sixteen
others on October 18, 1907. The edict of ban-
ishment seems to have been ignored, for he went

back to Hotevilla. Where else would he go, but back to his village where he belonged? He stayed there as long as he lived; all of which time he was 100 per cent Hostile, resenting and resisting with vigor every encroachment of the white man's culture. Superintendents came and Superintendents went, but each newcomer found Yokeoma there, a thorn in his side. He died in 1928 and directed that none should succeed him, especially not his son Dan. Dan was an active Traditionalist all his days.

Tewaquaptewa was stripped of his civil authority but permitted to retain his postion as Chief Priest. (In the Hopi way there is no division of church and state). He was given a choice: he could go away to school for three years for the purpose of learning to speak English and to become a better leader of his people, or he could go to prison for three years. He chose the first course.

Entry of Superintendent Lemmon, November, 1906:

Tewaquaptewa and Frank Seyumptewa and families (Tewaquaptewa took his wife and adopted daughter, Mina, child of his wife's sister) and twenty-two children of school age arrived at Sherman Institute. Whereupon the Chief discarded his village garb and donned the usual school uniform. Also had his hair trimmed

*within a day or two on his own request, and
applied for a hat. He falls in line with the rest
of the pupils and attends school regularly.*

*We have placed the married men and their
families in two large rooms, which adjoin, and
they seem happy. Tewaquaptewa does not wish
to attend religious services.*

Tewaquaptewa did learn to speak English
but not much about chieftainship. He soon tired
of school and ceased to go. When he returned
to his village, things were never the same again.
The village was slowly disintegrating. Over half
of the former villagers now lived at Hotevilla,
and many of the Friendly families were moving
off to mesa to be closer to the government school
and to their land and water, making a new village called Kiakochomovi, or New Oraibi. The
close-knit traditions that had given the Chief
his influence were broken, members of clans and
families were on opposite sides, and Tewaquaptewa was Chief in name only.

The snake dance has not been held in Oraibi
since 1906. Perhaps some principal priest left,
taking with him the rights and paraphernalia
of his office and the secrets of his clan. No one
had the authority to initiate the younger men
into the societies. Initiation into higher priesthood covers a period of over a year. The fact that
the young boys were away at school and could

not be indoctrinated in their respective kiva cere-
monies weakened the hold of the traditions on
those who should have become the leaders.

The Chief saw his power gradually wane.
The Indian Agent tried various ways to bolster
up the chief image. He gave Tewaquaptewa a
position on the police force for one thing, but
the Chief did not measure up. He became an unhappy and quarrelsome old man in his tumble-
down village. His sole shadow of authority in
his later years was that tourists were required
to see him and pay him a fee of one dollar for
permission to see the village. He told them that
if they wanted to take pictures they must have
permission of the individual and pay him a fee.
Consent to have one's picture taken is given
reluctantly, because the Hopis think that each
time your picture is taken, it takes that much
time off your life. Tewaquaptewa carved kachina
dolls to sell. When he died in 1960, he left no
successor. He decreed that all ritual objects per-
taining to his office be buried with him, and this
was done.

To School in Keams Canyon

VERY EARLY ONE MORNING toward the end of October, 1906, we awoke to find our camp surrounded by troops who had come during the night from Keams Canyon. Superintendent Lemmon called the men together, ordering the women and children to remain in their separate family groups. He told the men it was a mistake to follow Yokeoma blindly; that the government had reached the limit of its patience; that the children would have to go to school. Yokeoma angrily defied them and refused to yield. He was taken to a house and put under guard.

All children of school age were lined up to be registered and taken away to school. Eighty-two children, including myself, were listed. It was late in the afternoon when the registration was completed. We were now loaded into wagons hired from and driven by our enemies, the Friendlies. There were not enough wagons, so the bigger boys had to walk. We were taken to the schoolhouse in New Oraibi, with military escort. We slept on the floor of the dining room that night.

The next morning three more wagons were hired, covered wagons drawn by four horses. All were loaded in, boys and girls in separate wagons. We just sat on the floor of the wagon, and still with military escort, started for Keams Canyon. In each wagon the older boys or girls looked after the little ones. I was one of the little ones. One little boy was about five years old. They let him live in the dormitory with the big girls so they could mother him. Everyone called him "Baby," and he was still called "Baby" when he was a grown man.

It was after dark when we reached the Keams Canyon boarding school and were unloaded and taken into the big dormitory, lighted with electricity. I had never seen so much light at night. I was all mixed up and thought it was daytime because it was so light. Pretty soon they gave us hardtack and syrup to eat. There were not enough beds, so they put mattresses on the floor. When I was lying down I looked up and saw where the light came from just before the matron turned out the lights.

For the next few days we were all curious about our new surroundings. We thought it was wonderful and didn't think much about home, but after a while, when we got used to the school, we got real homesick. Three little girls slept in a double bed. Evenings we would gather in a corner and cry softly so the matron would not hear and scold or spank us. I would try to be a comforter, but in a little while I would be crying too. I can still hear the plaintive little voices saying, "I want to go home. I want my mother." We didn't understand a word of English and didn't know what to say or do.

Our native clothing was taken away from us and kept in boxes until our people came to take them. We were issued the regular school clothes. Each girl had two every-day dresses, three petticoats, two pairs of underwear, two pairs of stockings, one pair of shoes, one Sunday dress, and two white muslin aprons to be worn over the dresses, except on Sunday. The dresses were of striped bed ticking, with gathered skirts and long sleeves.

Some of the Friendly girls and those from

other villages used to call us Hostiles and tease us until we would cry. At night when the doors were closed and locked and little girls were supposed to be in bed for the night, our tormentors would take our native clothes from the boxes and put them on and dance around making fun of us.

Boys and girls marched to the dining room from their separate dormitories. Usually the bigger boys got there first. Meals were served on twelve long tables, family style. Older boys and girls set the tables, and one of the older ones sat at the head of the table and served the food. There were Navajos there, even though it was a school for Hopis. It seemed a Navajo was always at the head and the Navajos would have their plates heaping full, while little Hopi girls just got a teaspoonful of everything. I was always hungry and wanted to cry because I didn't get enough food. They didn't give second helpings, and I thought I would just starve. You can't go to sleep when you are hungry.

In the center of the table was a big plate of bread. The big boys would grab it as they went in. By the time little boys and girls got in, there was no bread. Sometimes the big boys would even take bread away from the little ones. There was a matron who was supposed to watch, but she didn't seem to notice these things.

For breakfast we had oatmeal mush, without milk or sugar, and plain bread. The Navajos didn't like the mush, so they took the bread and we had the mush. At noon it was beef, potatoes, and gravy, with prunes or bread pudding for dessert. At night we had the leftovers, sometimes with beans. Another dish often served was salt bacon gravy over bread; bacon was fried in small pieces, flour was added and browned in the grease, water was added, and the mixture was boiled until it was thickened into gravy. Without the bread there wasn't much nourishment. Sometimes we little ones were hunger driven to ask the boys to give us just one slice of bread to go with our gravy, but they would never do it, so we just drank the gravy. Day after day, the food had a sameness. How we longed for some food cooked by our mothers — the kind and quantity we were used to eating.

On the few occasions when the girls did beat the boys to the dining room, we marched right in and did as they did. We took all the bread and piled it on our stools and covered it with our aprons, while we stood waiting until everyone was in place and the blessing on the food was said. Then we would pick up our bread and sit on the stools. Later on they changed the system, and instead of seating the boys on one side of the table and the girls on the other, girls of one age were put at tables by themselves, and the same for the boys. I fared better then.

When you were sick the matron put you to bed in the dormitory. She was sympathetic and tried to comfort you. She brought your meals on a tray, and there was enough food. The trouble was when you were sick you didn't feel like eating.

It seemed like everything was against us at first.

We were a group of homesick, lonesome, little girls, huddled together on the schoolgrounds early one morning, when we wondered what was making the approaching clinking sound. Running to the high, woven wire fence around the playground, we saw a long line of men walking down the road. They were some of the seventy or so fathers from Hotevilla who had been arrested for resisting the government and had been sentenced to ninety days of hard labor; the Superintendent was using them to improve and build a dug-way into the canyon, thereby shortening the route by several miles. Supplies for the military post and the school were hauled along this road, and the traders who came by team and wagon from Holbrook also used it. What a thrill as one little girl after another recognized her father and pressed against the fence, calling out to him.

The construction gang walked four miles out to the job every morning. They were fastened together in twos with ball and chain. If one didn't keep step with his partner he might fall down, but they would only laugh about it. They were not ashamed of their condition because they knew in their hearts they had done no wrong; they had only protested having their lives interfered with. An officer with a stick would see to it that they did not stop to talk to their little girls. After that, each morning we ran out to see if our fathers went by. We would cry if we saw them and cry if we didn't. I recognized my father in the chain gang only once. He was put on kitchen duty, and I saw him there once before he was sent to prison at Fort Huachuca.

Following is a letter from the wife of one of the prisoners at Keams Canyon. It is dated December 28, 1906, and addressed to the Agency Superintendent.

My husband raised corn at Oraibi this year, but he did not gather it because soldiers took him away. Horses and cattle ate up the corn. I have no beans, only the food they give me from the village. These women want to go to school and be with their husbands and have food. Even if the husbands return here at once it will not change the condition of poverty. A year must pass, another growing season, before we can grow crops.

Investigation showed that they had lost their crops and did need food, and some were taken to Keams Canyon.

Being a little girl and away at Keams Canyon, I hardly realized until later the very sad plight of my mother, along with the other exiles back at Hotevilla; there were seven old men and a handful of younger ones who had promised to cooperate, twenty-three children under school age, and sixty-three women — aged ones, middle-aged ones bereft of their children, and young mothers with little babies, all longing and crying for their old homes and fields and for their men folk and their children who had been taken away. Few had the strength to gather and chop wood and to bring in the water. Their corn baskets were empty. They were so hungry! Sometimes the younger women would organize a rabbit hunt. The best time for this is when snow is on the ground. They wrapped their feet in whatever was available; a piece of sheepskin with the wool inside is good if tied on securely. They had no guns, just rocks and sticks and maybe a dog. If your dog caught it, it was your rabbit. Somehow they managed to survive the winter, while I had three meals each day and a comfortable bed and a warm building to shelter me.

The months passed by, and then it was the last day of school that first year at Keams Canyon. Parents in wagons, on horseback, and burros converged on the campgrounds around the school, from all directions. They had come to take their children home for the summer. There were parents from Hotevilla, but they would not promise to bring us back to school in September, so I was left to spend the summer at the school along with other boys and girls of Hostile parentage.

During the summer we fared better in the dining room because there were only about twenty girls and six boys and no Navajos. The big girls who worked in the kitchen and dining room favored us. In the cellar behind the kitchen there were many sacks of potatoes. Sometimes one of the older girls on kitchen duty would slip a raw potato to us little girls. They tasted good and sweet. I have tasted raw potato many times, but have never found any that tasted as sweet.

Come September, 1907, all the other children were brought back to school by their parents, and we were back in the regular routine again. One October afternoon, our eyes followed a few government wagons as they wended their way down the dug-way into the canyon and stopped at the campgrounds, and lo! the cargo unloaded itself — men, the prisoners being returned from Fort Huachuca. They had come by train to Holbrook, and then by team and wagon on out to Keams Canyon. We watched as the men filed by on their way to the dining room to be fed, and what a thrill, I recognized my own father. He was dressed in an old military uniform and looked fine and young and straight to me, and I was proud of him.

We talked together for a little while that

night and again in the morning. My father's Hopi name is Talashongnewa, but he was given the name of Sam at Huachuca, and from then was known as Sam Talashongnewa. He didn't feel mean toward the soldier guards. He said they treated the Hopis well and were loved by them, and that many of them had tears in their eyes when they said "good-by" to their Indian prisoners. But the prisoners came back still Hostile. My father's attitude had not changed, and it was many years before he could even begin to tolerate any part of the white man's culture. The prisoners were released to walk the forty miles on home to Hotevilla; it probably seemed a short forty miles to them.

As soon as they could, which was a year after we were taken away to Keams Canyon, some of the mothers came to visit their children. They came in a burro caravan of eight to ten. If one did not own a burro she would borrow or hire one on which she packed blankets and food for herself and as much as she could load on of piki, parched corn, dried peaches, and the like to give to her children. Mothers who couldn't make the trip would send bundles to their children. These travelers got everything ready the night before so they could start early in the morning. It was a long day's journey. The women walked most of the way, each driving her burro before her.

When a woman got very tired she would stop the burro near a stump or rock and climb on and ride for a while.

Arriving at the school late, they found shelter in the rock rooms built by the big boys and slept in their own blankets and ate their own food during their stay. Meat was not expensive, and the school had lots of meat. If the cook was good natured, he would give a Hopi mother a bone with a little meat on it, which she could boil with her corn.

My mother did not come the first time — she came two times during the four years I was at Keams. I had a good godmother, a very nice one. She came every time and brought me food and even some bone dolls to play with. We thought we were sitting on top of the world to have our mothers with us for a little while and to have some food they had cooked over the camp-fire. After school they were permitted to come over and visit for a little while, bringing with them some parched corn or some piki. They usually stayed three days.

We learned by sad experience to have our housemother lock up our precious bundle of piki or parched corn, otherwise it would be pilfered. The matrons were usually older women who were pretty good to us. On the first visit, the mothers took home the native clothing that we were wearing at the time we were — shall we say — kidnapped.

I remember the first Christmas at Keams Canyon. We had never known about Christmas. In the evening, Mr. Lorenzo Hubbell, who had a trading post at Keams Canyon, and another man came to the dormitory with boxes of apples and oranges and hard candy. Mr. Hubbell got up on a table and called the girls to gather around. We were wearing our usual pinafore aprons. He said, "Hold out your aprons and catch." He threw oranges and apples and candy this way and that way. Some of the girls had their aprons loaded, and some got very little or none. I don't think he threw all of them, because as the girls filed out he looked into their aprons and for those who had just a little, he put some more into their pinafores. He just said, "This is for Christmas." I didn't know what they meant, and they didn't tell us any Christmas story.

The second year, Christmas was just the same as the year before, but I understood more of the English words. Later they had programs and songs. Always Mr. Hubbell furnished candy and oranges; later the government provided even toys. I remember a little doll that I got, and some play dishes. Once I got a very nice doll that came in a box from a group of children from the Baptist Church. The girl who sent the doll asked me to be a pen pal, and I wrote to her for a while. When I was bigger, we girls did sometimes exchange little gifts at Christmas time.

I had never had my hair braided and tied before I went to Keams Canyon to school. My mother brushed it with a brush she made from certain grasses she gathered for that purpose, but little Hopi girls went with their hair hanging loose. At first they give each girl a comb, as I remember it, but these combs were soon lost from our boxes. I had lots of hair and had never tried to comb it myself, so my first efforts didn't look so good, and the other girls laughed at me.

So, certain bigger girls were detailed to come and braid the hair of the little girls. Each school morning the girls would come in to the washroom early to do the hair combing. If you had a big sister, it was her duty to comb your hair. The girls liked to comb the hair of a pretty little girl. I was always the last one chosen. My long hair got matted and snarled, and they were rough, and it pulled. It was all combed the same way; parted in four sections with two braids on each side of the head; the crown section on one side was braided first and then merged into the braid down the back section.

Once a girl from Polacca, while combing my hair, said to me, "Will you give me something? If you don't I will pull your hair. Something like

piki or dried peaches that your mother brought."
I had to say "Yes," and give. Another said, "Give
me some of your parched corn. I know you have
some." I said, "I just have a little bit." She said,
"That is why I want it now, or you will have
nothing to give me." I didn't want to, but I had
to give.

So we little ones tried hard to learn to comb
our own hair. How I wished for a comb of my
own. Once I went into the lavatory and there
was a Navajo girl with a lot of long hair trying
to comb her hair with a coarse brush, like they
used for scrubbing the floors.

If, while having my hair combed, I put my
head down, crying a little because it pulled so
hard, the girl who was combing my hair would
jerk my head up by the hair. It was right then
that I began to think, "Why do big girls have
to pull little girls' hair and be mean to them?
When I grow up I will be kind to little girls."
And I remembered to do it. If I ever pulled their
hair when combing it, I didn't mean to do it.
When other girls would gang up on someone
who was not very popular, I always felt sorry
for the victim. Even at school some of the girls
were mean to me but would still come and ask
me to help them with a hard lesson; I always
helped them.

I was really serious at school, even from the
beginning, but some of the teachers were unkind

to me. Once when I gave the wrong answer, the teacher boxed me real hard on the ear. I had earache after that, every night for a long time, and I can't hear very well out of that ear. If they had boxed somewhere else it wouldn't have been so bad.

Every Saturday morning the little girls had to go outside the dormitory and stay out while the big girls cleaned the rooms, no matter how cold it was. The ground was often covered with snow, and it seemed like my feet would never get warm.

Every Saturday afternoon it was hair washing time. At the sound of the bell all the little girls went to the wash room where a matron would be in charge. We lined up — seems like that was the first English we learned, "Get in line, get in line," all the time we had to get in line. First, the delousing treatment. You dipped your fingers in bowls of kerosene, provided by the government, and applied it to hair and scalp. Next we lined up, and each had a fine-tooth comb run through her hair. If it came out clean you could shampoo and go out and play, but if the comb showed "nits" the word was, "Go to the buggy bench."

On the long bench we sat. More kerosene was applied, fine-tooth combs were passed out, and the girls combed each other's hair or just picked nits from the strands of hair. It seemed like we just had to sit there all afternoon when we wanted to go out and play. After a while the matron would inspect again and some would be given a clean pass, and a bar of yellow laundry soap with which to wash the hair. It washed the kerosene out all right and helped to keep the lice away. Some of the girls were not eager workers and in desperation the matron would say, "Go on out and play, but next week you will still be on the buggy bench."

Most of our teachers were women. There was a certain teacher, a man, who when the class came up to "read," always called one of the girls to stand by him at the desk and look on the book with him while the others took their turns at reading, down the line. He would put his arms around and fondle this girl, sometimes taking her on his lap. Some of the girls seemed to like it. They laughed, and neither teacher nor pupil paid any attention the reading.

I was scared that I would be the one next called to his desk. Finally I was. He called, "Helen, come to the desk while we read." When I got there, Mr. M put his arm around me and rubbed my arm all the way down. He rubbed his face against mine. When he put his strong whiskers on my face, I screamed and screamed and didn't stop until he let me go. I knew he was embarrassed. I ran out of the room before he could catch me, and to the dormitory.

They didn't punish me. When they saw me they knew I was really scared. I didn't go back to school that day and they didn't force me. The other girls said his face was red all the rest of the day.

One summer day several of us were playing with our bone dolls. One little girl reenacted the expulsion of the Hostiles from Oraibi. She was so realistic in her dramatization that all the other girls left their own play and came to watch. She built up sand for the flat-roofed houses and placed sticks there for the women, naming them and mocking for them as the Hostile families trailed across the plaza and out of the village.

One, two, three, and four years passed by, and each spring we girls from Hotevilla saw the children from the other villages go home with their parents for the summer, while we were kept at school. I was four years older and not one of the little girls any more, when, one fine day in June, 1910, all the girls and boys from the Hostiles were smiling. Our fathers had been busy building houses and opening up cornland. Toward the end of June their hearts were turned to their children in Keams Canyon, and they came, riding burros, asking permission to take their children home for two weeks to be there at the Home Dance. The Superintendent was a pleasant man and gave his consent, with the understanding that our parents would bring us back when school started on September first.

We made quite a caravan, about fifty boys and girls, each riding a burro, with the fathers walking beside us, all happy to be going home. It was a long day's journey. When the trail was rocky and steep we got off and walked. When we came to a flat valley, there would be racing to see whose burro could run the fastest; our fathers ran along, keeping up with us. It was dark when we got to the new village. Rock houses had replaced the makeshift shelters we had left. Things were different, but our mothers were there and we were home again.

When September came in 1910, our fathers did not take us back to Keams Canyon to school. I spent a year at home and enjoyed the old life, learning from my mother the things a Hopi girl should know.

Home for One Year

Grinding the corn is the most important homemaking skill. This is not a simple task. First of all one must have the equipment. The "mata" is about twelve by eighteen inches. A family usually has one mata for coarse grinding and more than one for fine grinding. The "matake," which is moved by the hands, is as long as the mata is wide, with rounded edges. These stones are prized and are passed from mother to daughter, or they are quarried and brought home to be shaped and smoothed by many hours of hard rubbing with other stones until they are smoothed.

The grinding area is a built-in fixture, so placed that as the woman kneels to grind, she faces the room. If there are many daughters in a family, there may be five or six grinding boxes in a row. The mata rests at a forty-degree angle in a box about two by two and a half feet across, and eight inches deep. These boxes used to be made of sandstone plastered with clay; some cornmeal was mixed with the top layer of the plaster and it hardened like cement and would not rub off. Nowadays the boxes are made of lumber.

The worker takes a small handful of corn from the left compartment of the box with one hand, holding the matake in the other; she places the corn on the mata, bounces the matake to crack the corn, and it falls to the bottom of the box. The cracked corn is swept up with a grass brush and brought back again and again for regrinding. When the grist is medium fine and there is about ten pounds, it is roasted in an earthen kettle (now iron kettles are used) which has a rounded bottom. The kettle is heated over coals outside or in the fireplace, and the woman stirs fast all the time with a stick or a little plaque until the grist smells like parched corn. Now it is returned to the grinding box and ground repeatedly until it is quite fine, when it is sifted through a woven basket (now a sieve) to remove the hulls. Then it goes back for a series of final grinding. As the meal gets finer the grinding goes slower; the flour feels moist from the oil in it and it sticks to the hands a little. The finished product is as fine as mill-ground flour. The texture varies with each individual; lazy women have coarser meal. If the grinder is a youngster of six years, she will do well to make a cupful in an hour, while her mother will do much more. Twenty-five pounds would be a pretty good day's work. The muscles of the torso become hard and strong from this work.

All daughters in the family grind. You don't grind just a little while before you cook a meal, you work all the daylight hours. Girls take pride in filling storage bowls and rounding them over the top; it is a sort of contest, who can make the most in a week. These filled bowls are stored on a shelf made by logs fastened into the wall, close together and near the ceiling, so the mice can't get it. You use from one end and use the oldest first. When it is time for festivals there will be enough and to spare. After that there is the second mile, to grind for an aunt who has no daughters. If a neighbor comes to roast her corn on your fire she brings her own wood. If a girl friend comes to visit, you don't play around. You grind. She may bring her own corn to grind as you talk. Mothers and daughters and neighbors talk and laugh and sing grinding songs composed for this purpose.

They say no man will marry a girl unless she can make piki. This household art I learned while I was at home that year. Piki is paper thin bread made from fine cornflour; it tastes like cornflakes and is really the forerunner of cornflakes. It will keep a long time if stored clean and dry. It is like bread with a meal, and is delicious with milk as a bowl of cereal, or as a cooky for a hungry child.

First comes the making of the piki stone. The men go to the quarry and bring back slabs of granite stone two to three inches thick and about eighteen by twenty-four inches. The wife does the smoothing and polishing. It takes long hours and many days, rubbing and rubbing with coarse hard rock and ending with very fine smooth pebbles, to wear the stone good and smooth.

The piki room may be a part of the house or a little room by itself. A foundation of rocks about a foot high is laid in grill fashion with an open end for wood for the fire, and the stone is placed thereon. A fireplace-like chimney carries the smoke from the fire out of the room. A little pit about eighteen inches deep is dug for the feet of the piki maker to add to her comfort as she sits on a sheepskin before the piki stone. The final step is the firing of the stone. A fire is kept burning all day long. When the stone becomes red hot, watermelon or muskmelon seeds which have been roasted until the hull becomes soft, and then ground fine, are sprinkled thickly over the stone. As the ground seed burns, it turns black and is rubbed over the surface with a thick folded rag. This is repeated over and over as the stone cools. The oil from the seed oozes out and penetrates and saturates the stone, and it turns black and shiny.

Before the stone cools too much, a little piki batter is made to try it out, to see if the stone is cured right. If it is, the piki will peel off easily the first time and the stone is ready and will last a long, long time — if you take good care of it. At the end of each piki-making, the stone is thoroughly oiled with animal fat. The next time the stone is used it is washed with soap weed and well rinsed.

Having ground her corn ahead of time, the housewife gets ready to spend a day making piki. First she must make a fire under the stone. It takes some time for the stone to heat, and while it is heating the batter is prepared as follows:

Into a big bowl put about four pounds of corn flour ground very fine. Into a small dish put a handful of clean greasewood ashes and pour boiling water over it. Divide the flour into two parts — three-fourths and one-fourth — pressing the smaller portion against the side of the bowl. Scald the big portion with boiling water. Strain the ash liquid through a whisk broom into the scalded flour and stir it with a stick until it sticks together in a soft dough. Knead the remaining one-fourth part into this mixture until it is smooth and all the lumps are out and it has cooled off somewhat. Adding a little water at a time, continue kneading and stirring until it has become a very thin batter. (Of course before you start this kneading, you wash your hands.) The ashes give the piki a delicate flavor and a light blue color.

The woman takes her bowl of batter to the piki stone and makes herself comfortable, with feet in the little pit, sheepskin to sit on, sticks of wood handy, and at her right the bowl and mats ready for the freshly baked cereal. The stone is tested for temperature and oiled by burning some melon seed and rubbing it in. A small piece of a sheep spinal cord that has been cooked and dried makes good grease for the stone. Piki should be baked with as little grease as possible so it will keep longer. After cooking each sheet of piki, the oiled rag is rubbed over the stone; when the piki does not peel readily, then the spinal cord is used.

The housewife dips her right hand into the batter and brings out about a teaspoonful and quickly brushes it over the stone, repeating until the stone is covered. As the piki cooks it peels up from the edge and the thin sheet is lifted off (the first one is discarded). A finished sheet is placed over the one that is cooking. As the second one cooks, the steam that it gives off softens the one on top, which is now quickly folded and rolled into a long narrow roll about two by eight inches. The sheet is finished and laid on the mat. The process continues endlessly, and the rolls are piled high. At the end of the making, the piki is stored away.

Sometimes I would grind for two or three days and get enough fine flour to make several big bowls of piki so I could have a generous supply. My eldest son Wayne was a little boy in Hotevilla and he would gather his friends and bring them home and want me to give each one of them some fresh piki. It is very good when fresh and warm. The boys would eat it as fast as I could make it. I would finally have to tell them, "You have had enough. Go out and play."

It is a lucky girl who inherits a piki stone from her mother. Sometimes a woman whose family is grown will make a stone in her free hours. This she may give to her daughters-in-law or even sell it to a young wife for as much as forty dollars, or trade it.

Mutton fat was the chief shortening in older days. It was used sparingly. Watermelon seeds were another source. We would save all the seeds from the melons and at the end of summer might have as much as twenty-five pounds of them. They are loaded with oil, principally used on the piki stone. Another use, however, is in making succotash. We cooked dry beans and hominy. The melon seeds are roasted and ground and then soaked in hot water. The oil comes out into the water, which is strained into the succotash when it is nearly cooked. It gives a good, nutty flavor to the dish. Now the younger housewives just use a spoonful of peanut butter for the flavor.

Parched corn is prepared outside over the coals. A round-bottomed iron kettle is placed at an angle over the coals, so that when the corn pops it hits the upper side of the kettle and falls back in. A cupful of clean sand is heated in the kettle before a handful of corn is added. The woman stirs rapidly, and the sand heats the corn on all sides and it cooks through. The sand is sifted out of the corn back into the kettle. While the corn is hot, salted water, handy in a dish nearby, is sprinkled over it. Nearly every kernel splits and is crisp and salted. Sometimes a little girl gets frightened and runs when her corn begins to pop, and her mother has to come and finish. Parched corn is delicious and keeps a long time. It is good for a snack or to carry on a journey, and it has many other uses.

It was while I was at home this time that my mother told me about the sex side of life, although even when I was younger she had not neglected that subject. She didn't try to make it sound nice nor beat about the bush but told me in plain language so I would understand. When my sister was married and my mother went to help at her wedding ceremony, I was quite young. She told me then, "Never sleep away from me, even in the same house with your father and brothers. If I am away overnight you sleep in the bed with your grandmother."

When a girl starts menstruating, then her mother teaches her the Hopi moral code, which is that she is to keep herself a virgin until she is married — that before marriage it is wrong, but at the time of her marriage it is right and proper. If she is attacked by a man she is to fight real hard and never yield, and a properly placed kick will stun a man for a while. After marriage, be true to your husband as long as you live. It will make a much better marriage if a girl keeps herself morally clean. It might break up your marriage if your man finds out that your past life has been bad. Even so, you would have to spend your life in the hereafter together.

Mothers caution little girls to avoid bodily

contact with boys, even their brothers, because the urge or desire is stronger in a man than in a woman, and to put your arms around him will awaken the desire. So when Hopi young people dance, they do not hold hands or touch each other. In most ceremonial dances a man dresses and takes the part of the woman dancer.

In the butterfly dance, the unmarried girl chooses her partner, who must be her cousin. The group practices for several weeks, which is, in a way, matchmaking with others of the dancers. Sometimes when the song says they hold hands, they do it. So you see why your older ones are opposed to school dances and parties where boys and girls dance with their arms around each other. A Hopi girl does not mingle with boys alone, even in the daytime. If there is a social, the girls walk together and the boys follow in a group serenading as they go.

A girl wears her hair long and loose until she is fourteen or fifteen years old. After she menstruates, she puts her hair up in two whorls at each side of her head, which shows her status as a woman. I should say her hair is put up for her. She can't do it herself. When a girl thus binds her hair she is supposed to act like a young lady — not walk alone in the streets nor talk loud, but stay at home and be industrious in learning to cook and care for the home and to be a good wife.

Some girls are married at the age of sixteen, but many wait until they are twenty or twenty-five or even thirty, so as to limit the size of their families. In olden days girls did not marry young. Very few who were not married had babies in my day.

In my time, if a young man wished to court a young lady, he was allowed to call at her house where he would stand outside, looking in through a small window. First the girl learned who was calling. If she liked him she would carry on a conversation. If she didn't like him, she would ignore him. The parents could lock the door and go to bed, but if things got too quiet, if the girl stopped grinding for too long, the mother would come to investigate.

The Hopi marriage is not for this life only but extends into life after death and cannot be put asunder. If a man or woman loses his or her mate through death or divorce and if there is a second marriage, the proper way is to marry someone who has also been married before. This is known, in the case of a man, as a "borrowed wife," who has been borrowed for this life.

Should a widow or a widower marry one who has never been married, the one who is marrying for the first time is said to have "put a burden on his (or her) back." That is, in life after death, the offender will be obliged to carry a big burden basket filled with rocks forever. The basket will rest on the back and be held by a strap around the forehead, which will in time wear a groove into the skull, while the deceased spouse will claim his original partner throughout eternity.

During the years when the fathers were away, there was continued hunger in Hotevilla. It took some time afterward to open new land to raise enough food. The year I was home we never did have enough food. Our scant harvest was nearly depleted when one morning late in May (1911) my mother awakened me early. We were going to Oraibi to shell corn for a cousin who would then give us some. We hurried on without breakfast, Mother carrying two-year-old Henry. We went straight to the cousin's house, only to find the door closed and locked. After a while Mother said we would come back another day. Another cousin invited us in for piki and some water, and we started home. I picked wild flowers for Mother, but she wasn't interested. When at last we arrived home and opened the door, there on the table was a big basket piled high with corn, and a dish-pan of white wheat flour and some baking powder. Mother broke down and cried as we literally caressed those ears of corn and that beautiful flour. Mother immediately made tortillas, and we ate.

Back to School

THE FOLLOWING SEPTEMBER (1911) the children from Hotevilla were gathered up by soldiers and again loaded into wagons and taken back to school. Some of the older girls had married, and some mothers combed the hair of their older daughters like a married woman does and dressed them like a married woman so that they were not taken back to Keams Canyon. From then on the children of the Hostiles were kept at school the year round.

There had been a change — a new Superintendent had come while we were away. The new man was hard-boiled. He said to us, "If I had my way you would never see your homes again. You would live like white people." We noticed some changes, some for the better.

Each older girl was assigned to a work detail — some in the kitchen or dining room, some in the laundry or cleaning the dormitories. Some worked in the morning and went to school in the afternoon, and vice versa. My first assignment was bathroom detail.

The bathroom was a big room in the basement. There was a long row of seats over a metal trough, with a big flush thing at one end. It "went off" automatically at intervals and made a lot of noise. At first I was afraid of it and afraid to go in and clean. I scrubbed it with soap and brush. I poured water on the cement floor and swept it with a broom. The two tubs and, later, showers were in another room and were not my detail.

Every three months we would be called together, and someone would read off the duties for each girl for the next three months. How I wanted to get out of being in that old bathroom all the time. I hoped I might get to wait tables in the dining room, maybe. When she read, "Helen, bathroom," I could have cried. I never did get a change.

Years afterward I met the woman who used

to be in charge of detail duty and asked her why I always had to have that assignment, and she said, "I will tell you why. No one else would keep it clean like you did, my dear."

One time, one of the boys planted a big patch of beans near the wash across from the school. The matron told several of us girls, "You go and pick those beans." Three refused to go, including little Helen. The matron insisted, and we got stubborn and said the beans belonged to the boy. She said that they were on the school grounds, but we wouldn't go with the other girls to pick the beans. It was the boy's father who had done the work and taken care of the bean patch. Imagine how he felt when he came to harvest his beans.

My mother came to visit me at school in the spring of 1912, the year after I had been at home. I remember it so well. She carried her baby, Lawrence, on her back as she walked or jogged along on her donkey. The baby had been born in September after I left for school. My mother was a very nice person. She stayed only a couple of days. They let her come into the basement of the dormitory. She had boiled corn and jerky which she cooked. It was hot and tasted so good. The next year she came, and Verlie came with her baby to show me, too.

We who stayed at school all the year round

had more training than the other girls. The teachers and matrons gave us responsibility and depended upon us as we grew older. When I was fifteen, I was in charge of the post laundry during the summer. This served the teachers and other government employees. It was a big job and hard work doing up white shirts with pleated fronts and stiff starched collars, and equally starched white, cotton dresses. The washing machines were big ones and were run by steam from the power house. The irons were heated on a wood stove. I ran the machines and had experience in sorting and checking the bundles. I was paid fifteen dollars a month.

What I earned myself was the only money I ever had. We were so poor that my parents didn't send me any money. Sometimes I worked in the homes of government employees. We were allowed to piece quilt tops from the leftover scraps from the sewing department. These we might sell at the post for fifty to seventy-five cents, or send home to our mothers. In the fall we would go out and gather piñon nuts to store for winter and maybe have some to sell.

One Navajo woman used to come to the school bringing juniper berries that she had gathered. We would save a piece of bread or meat or gingerbread from our meal and take it into the yard and exchange with her for a handful of berries. They were big and purple like grapes and very sweet, though full of seeds. After the noon meal, this woman might have a good-sized pile of food, which she would wrap in her kerchief and take home to feed her family. Then she gathered more berries for the next day's barter.

I enjoyed school and was eager to learn. I was a good reader and got good grades. The teachers favored me and whenever visitors came they always called on me to recite. I was not the most popular girl in school and my ability did not help me socially, it only made the others jealous. The girls would get me out in the yard and say, "You are quite an important person in the classroom, but out here you are nothing." I would answer, "Isn't that what we are here for, to learn?" I tried not to be mean to anyone but still I was not favored among the students. The boys razzed me about my work in school too; I really wasn't very good looking, that might have been a part of it, but I could only carry on.

I was a wallflower. When there were parties or dances, I sat back in the corner with another girl and watched. No one would dance with us. One dance night we both got dressed like the rest of the girls. We lined up to go out, and the matron stood at the door and watched the girls go out. We took our places at the end of the line, and when she wasn't looking we slipped into the clothing room. The matron locked the door and followed the last girl out and walked with them over to the dining room where they usually had the dance. While she was gone, we changed our clothes and ran up the two flights of stairs to the bedrooms; from there we watched the dancing and maybe wished a little. This worked very well so we did it several times until we were found out.

In the spring and again in the fall we had a picnic. The girls and boys walked in separate groups, while our lunches were taken in a wagon. It was good to be out of school, outside the fence, and feel free again.

Ella's father had lost his mind. I think this was at the bottom of what happened that summer night in the dormitory. The Hopi girls were all housed in one dormitory during the summer. Ella was about fourteen years old. Maybe one of the girls didn't like her or was afraid of her. Anyway we were all in our long-sleeved, flannel nightgowns getting into bed, when one girl said she heard a noise under her bed. She said she didn't see anything but heard this horrible noise and that the noise went toward Ella's bed, that Ella was a witch and had changed herself into a ghost and gotten under the bed to scare us. They ganged up on Ella and said that everyone should pass by Ella and give her a hard sock on the back.

I wouldn't do it. After everyone had hit Ella, the girls who had been holding her by the arms let her go. She had taken the blows without a murmur, but when they let her go, Ella ran screaming downstairs and told the matron. She said, "Everyone of them did it except Little Helen." (There was another Helen in school known as Big Helen.) The matron came right up and put us all into bed and warned that the next morning all would be severely punished — except Little Helen. My, I felt little that night. I got into bed right away and covered up my head so they wouldn't stare at me.

For punishment, the girls had to clean the whole, big dormitory building. They worked all day, washing the walls and ceilings and all the windows, while Ella and I walked leisurely around the yards. I knew Ella did not do it; she was not a witch. The poor girl had no friends; it made me feel sad and sorry for her. I wanted to be her friend.

After this they called her "Ella Ghost" all the time right to her face. I was still friendly with Ella all through the summer. We would walk together or play with our bone dolls under a tree. My girl friends would say, "Why don't you come away from Ella Ghost and play with us?" After a while it died down, and when school started and the others came back, Ella found herself another friend. Ella was always an unhappy girl, even after her marriage. She died early.

When I was about twelve years old I had a friend, Amelia Albert. We played and imagined ourselves as two eastern society women. Amelia was Mrs. Judson of New York City. She had a son and a daughter. I was Mrs. Holmes of Philadelphia and had two sons and a daughter. We got our ideas from books we had read. We wrote letters to each other telling about our families.

We would find hard words in a book and look them up in the dictionary, see what they meant and use them in our letters. We would try to be like society women. When we met I would say, "Good morning, Mrs. Judson. I am so glad to see you. Have you read such and such a book?" It was fun 'and helped us a lot in our English. Amelia would always write "no" for "know" and I was always reminding her.

One day in school the teacher caught me in the act of passing a letter to Amelia, and she took the paper from me. I was telling in detail about the coming-out party of my daughter and describing the dress she would wear.

When the teacher took my letter, I surely felt humble. I was afraid I would be punished, but I wasn't. First chance she had the teacher read the letter, and all morning long she had a smile on her face. During recess I saw her letting the other teachers read the letter of Mrs. Holmes to Mrs. Judson, and everyone laughed. My teacher gave me a good grade in English composition because of that letter.

Sunday was a busy day at boarding school. We had to go to Sunday School where we were separated into age groups for Bible instruction. Different churches came and held services. We were required to go to evening services too.

I remember one preacher especially, although they were all about the same. I couldn't understand a thing he was talking about but had to sit and listen to a long sermon. I hated them and felt like crying. If I nodded my head going to sleep, a teacher would poke me and tell me to be good. It seemed as if this preacher would talk all night. He put a great deal of emotion into his sermons. He would work himself up to a climax talking loud and strong, and then calm down to a whisper, and I would think, "Now he is going to stop." But no, he would start all over again and go on and on.

The different sects were always urging and bribing us with little presents to join their church. It didn't appeal to me and I didn't join any of them.

One year there were three Navajo girls at the school. They were sort of prisoners because they had gotten married too young, "they" said.

They were under careful watch. They were big girls and looked about seventeen or eighteen years old. One of the girls learned a little English and mixed with us and didn't seem to want to go home. The other two must have been married for some time, for they were sullen and kept to themselves all the time, wanting to go home to their husbands.

One Saturday morning when we were out on the playground, our attention was drawn to the yard of the main office where many Navajos, among them many policemen, had ridden up on horses. We could not hear them but concluded they were talking loud, because of the violent gesturing. Then one policeman dismounted and, stepping forward, took off the shirt of his uniform and threw it on the ground at the feet of the Superintendent. Next he stripped off his pants and followed with his cap and belt and gun, and threw them on the ground before the Superintendent. He had other clothes on under his uniform. Then he jumped on his horse and snatched the bridle of an extra horse standing conveniently nearby, and went galloping down to the bottom terrace below the schoolgrounds. I had noticed the two Navajo girls sitting on the lowest step of the lowest terrace, each holding in her hand a little kerchief-tied bundle and watching the commotion in front of the main office.

When the policeman started toward the

girls, they stood up. He stopped in front of them, took the hand of one girl and helped her mount behind him on the horse, while the second girl leaped to the back of the second horse. We all watched as they raced up the canyon, to freedom? When we turned our eyes back to the group of men the crowd was dispersing. Nobody made any effort to go after the runaways. The Navajo policemen did not want to bring the girls back.

Phoenix Indian School

TIME PASSED BY, and I grew older, and it was better for me at school. I was weaned away from home. The girls from the other mesas gradually became more friendly. The twenty or so of us who stayed at school all summer became close friends. The teachers and everyone treated us pretty well.

At the end of the school year in 1915 I had finished the sixth grade, which was as far as one could go at Keams Canyon. I wanted to go somewhere else and continue my schooling. I could not go without the consent of my parents, which they would not give. I was joined by a few others of like mind, and we begged the Superintendent, Mr. Leo Crane, to let us go to Phoenix Indian School. We even suggested, "You could say we are a little older than we are." He finally agreed to let us go on our own responsibility.

That summer another girl and I were trusted to go home on our own promise not to do what our parents told us, and to come back in two weeks. We said to each other, "We will humor our parents. We will do what they want; dress in Hopi traditional clothes; let them fix our hair in whorls while we are there, anything to please them." I had lived at the school so long that it seemed like my home. I stayed with my parents in Hotevilla only ten days and went back to the dormitory at Keams Canyon.

Dr. Breid (the same doctor who took care of Emory when he fell over the cliff at Keams Canyon) was now the school doctor and also the assistant to Superintendent Brown at Phoenix Indian School. He came to Keams Canyon to make the arrangements and supervise the trip of the Indian boys and girls to Phoenix in the fall of 1915. It took two days by team and wagon to Holbrook, with boys and girls in separate wagons. From there we went by train — about seventy of us, all in one car — to Flagstaff, Ash

Fork, Prescott, and finally Phoenix. A matron traveled with us.

Emory met us at the train in Phoenix, but I didn't know it. He had been assigned by Dr. Breid to meet the train and escort the boys, walking from the Santa Fe depot on Fourth Avenue over to the streetcar line on Second Street and Washington, where he supervised their boarding the streetcar and rode out, way out, to the Indian School.

Emory rode to the depot with Dr. Breid in his two-seated surrey with fringe on top. I was one of the four girls whom Dr. Breid invited to ride with him in his buggy out to the Indian School. As they came to the administration building the new students were met by the school band, a military type of welcome. The students were formed into lines and marched to their assigned dormitories to the music of the band.

It was a military school. We marched to the dining room three times a day to band music. We arose to a bell and had a given time for making our beds, cleaning our rooms, and being ready for breakfast. Everything was done on schedule, and there was no time for idleness.

Our clothing was furnished by the government. We had long black stockings and heavy black shoes, but the dresses were of good material made in the sewing room to fit individually. Some of the bigger girls worked about the town doing housework on Saturday and bought their own dress shoes when they could. We went to school half a day and worked half a day.

The home economics department had a big production room where all girls' clothing and shirts for the boys were made, and we did a lot of sewing there. Besides this sewing the girls were assigned to laundry and home-cleaning details. The boys were put on janitor work, caring for the premises and learning shop skills. The school had a dairy (where the Veteran's Hospital now is). The boys took care of the cows and did the milking, and the girls learned to care for the milk.

Sunday morning all pupils had to be in their uniforms and stand for inspection at 7:30. All lined up outside their buildings and stood at attention while being inspected by the principal, head matron, head disciplinarian, and the doctor. The boys gave a military salute as the officers passed, and the girls held out their hands to be inspected. The officers noticed every detail and would say, "Your shoe string is not tied right," "Your hands are dirty," or "Your shoes do not shine." Following inspection we marched to the auditorium for church services.

At first I was homesick for Keams Canyon, but it soon wore off. During the very first week Superintendent Brown (of the Indian School) came looking for two girls to work in his home.

I was one chosen. I was paid five dollars a month. The Brown family consisted of a grown son, away at school, and daughters aged thirteen, eleven, and seven. I was sixteen. I was required to sleep at the dormitory. Sometimes after I had eaten in the dining room Mrs. Brown would want me to come back and help in the kitchen in the evening and I would get to eat twice. Sometimes she would save a piece of pie or cake for me.

Clara, the other girl in the Brown home, had always been given the shirts to iron while I did the plain pieces, but when Clara was sick for a week Mrs. Brown found out that I could do fancy ironing too. She let me run the whole house when she saw that I could do it. It was the policy to have the girls change assignments every few months, but Mrs. Brown always wanted me back. They treated me like one of the family and took me with them when they went for a ride in their Ford car. I enjoyed riding out to orchards for fruit and to farms for vegetables. They even took me a few times on weekend camping trips. I worked for them during the summer the first year. After two years with the Browns, the matron decided it would be good for me to have other experience so she put me in the sewing room where the older girls made the school clothing.

School life was obnoxious to many students, and discipline was military style. Corporal punishment was given as a matter of course; whipping with a harness strap was administered in an upstairs room to the most unruly. One held the culprit while another administered the strap. Girls were not often whipped, but one big Yuma girl grabbed the strap and chased both the matron and the disciplinarian from the room. Sometimes boys and even girls would run away, even though they were locked in at night, they managed to get out somehow. Often a boy and a girl would have it planned and go at the same time. They would usually start to go home. Older boys with records of dependability would be sent to find and bring them back. Emory was often sent. He would go to town on the streetcar and look around the streets, but sometimes they would get as far away as Glendale or Peoria. Then Emory would have to go by train, and when he found them bring them back and deliver the boys to their disciplinarian and the girls to the matron. Punishment for the girls might be cleaning the yards, even cutting grass with scissors, while wearing a card that said, "I ran away." Boys were put in the school jail, a small adobe house with high windows. Repeaters had their heads shaved and had to wear a dress to school. Some of them forgot how to wear pants.

One family from Camp Verde had children on the road most of the time. Sam, the eldest, left his dress on the doorstep of the house of the disciplinarian and went home. Another time he took his younger brother out of the hospital, discarding the hospital garb and going "as is." This was later than my time. In World War II Sam received a recognition for outsmarting the "Japs" in the jungles of the South Pacific, running communication wires, so his training did not go for naught.

I still loved to study and learn. I had to earn all of my spending money and my hands were never still. I was always doing embroidery or crochet or tatting, making things to sell. I had learned to be careful and never spend my money for things I did not need. In the three years that I was in Phoenix I never bought candy or pop but bought thread to make things so I could earn more.

We would shop at Korrick's, going to town on Saturday afternoon by streetcar. A teacher would be responsible for about thirty girls for an afternoon. Some would go to a show, some would shop at the dime stores. They got to know us at Korrick's and let us have our handwork supplies at a discount. One of my Hopi friends did beautiful embroidery work. They put one of her pieces on display in the store. The saleslady and even the manager would visit with us. We enjoyed learning new skills.

One-third to one-half of the students stayed at the school during the summertime. Some did not have a home to go to, and then there were us Hopis with parents still Hostile. The boys worked at construction of new buildings, in the school dairy and poultry farm, or in the vegetable garden. Some of the girls were placed in fine homes that had been checked by the school; sometimes it would be the lady they had worked for on Saturday during the school year. It was nice if you had a friend who worked near you. Perhaps a hostess was serving a big dinner. Then I would go and help my friend Millie pour from a big bottle into lots of little glasses, wash dishes, or do other kitchen chores. One time my lady, Mrs. Scott, was going to be gone for a weekend. She said, "You may kill two chickens and cook dinner for your friends." This is what I did during my second summer in Phoenix.

The third and last summer I worked again for Mrs. Scott, who had asthma. She left everything for me to do. I even made shirts for her husband and son. We spent most of the time at Ironsprings. She treated me very well. When I decided to go home she said, "If you will stay with me one more year I will give you a sewing machine when you get married." I didn't stay.

Mr. Brown retired from the Phoenix Indian School superintendency in 1934. Nearly every summer, until his death, Mr. and Mrs. Brown came to visit us on the reservation. When Mrs. Brown was left alone and her health was failing, she planned on coming to live with me. I would have been glad to care for her and be good to her, but first she went to visit her daughters in the East. She was senile and they put her in an institution.

One evening I was in the Brown kitchen doing the dishes when the doorbell rang. One of the Brown daughters went to the door and then came to the kitchen and said, "It is for you." When I got to the door there stood Emory with a package in his arms. I was so glad to see someone from home that I guess I lit up as I stepped out onto the porch to take the bundle from him and thank him, and we talked a little. (P.S. Emory has been the light in my life ever since.)

At the request of Mrs. Brown, I had written my folks to send me a bundle of the native grass that we used to make brushes for our hair. My mother, learning that Emory was going back to Phoenix the next day, made a bundle of the grass and a little piki. She didn't have time to parch corn or get anything else to send.

Emory was older and one of the trusted upperclassmen, having already been in school in Phoenix for three years, and I had admired him from afar. He had a girl in Bacabi and had expected to marry her. When he went home that summer, he found his girl married to someone else, so he came back to Phoenix school and soon started noticing other girls. When we met on campus he would stop and talk to me. At the school socials and lawn parties we would be together. We didn't see each other much at school because with the split sessions our classes didn't coincide. Many of the girls wanted Emory. I couldn't understand why he chose me. I had always been a wallflower, and Emory was the best looking (and the best) boy in school. When we would read the story of the ugly duckling in our school reader, I always thought of myself as the ugly duckling. Now it was like the story; I felt like a beautiful swan. We were meant for each other, you can tell.

There was a drug and grocery store across from the Indian School. Boys had more freedom to leave the campus than girls did. When we did not like the food in the dining room, if we had money, we did not eat there, but would ask the boys to buy something for us at the store.

Emory worked at the power plant that produced heat for the dormitories and school buildings and made the ice and electricity for the whole institution. He was responsible for keeping the generators running. Some of the boys worked under Emory's supervision, learning to be power plant operators. The school employees often brought their cars to him to work on after school hours. Motors were not as complicated then as now. During the summer months Emory would enter into contract with farmers to furnish hands for harvesting crops, mostly hay and cantaloupes. He would be responsible to the school for the boys who went to out to work. They would find a place near a farm, maybe the barn, where they could sleep if the farm were a long way from the school, like out at Glendale. They were fed by the farmer. They hauled the crops with team and wagon, and the hay was baled with horse power.

After three years I had completed the eighth grade and should have been graduated, but that year there were no graduates. They moved graduation up to the tenth grade. We went slowly because we did book work only half a day. We had to go through 6B-6A, 7B-7A, and so on. I started in 7B.

Three years was the maximum time you could stay without the consent of your parents. Superintendent Brown said that I could go home or stay on, the choice was mine. But my three years were up, and something told me to go home. However, I planned to go home for a visit only and then go away to high school and learn good English. Then, as I already knew the laundry business, I would go back to Keams Canyon and start a laundry and have all the Reservation business.

So in September, 1918, my best friend Selma and I used the money we had earned during the summer and went by train to Holbrook and on to Keams Canyon by mail truck. Here we were delayed for two weeks. The mail to Hotevilla was carried in a buckboard, and there was no room for passengers. We worked for two weeks at Keams until the mail carrier came with a wagon and we could go on to Hotevilla.

Home After Thirteen Years

I DIDN'T FEEL at ease in the home of my parents
now. My father and my mother, my sister and
my older brother told me to take off those clothes
and wear Hopi attire. My brother gave me two
complete Hopi costumes that he had woven
especially for me, nice and fine and warm and
scratchy. I didn't wear them, and Verlie was
after me all the time about it. She finally said,
"Since you won't wear the clothes that your
brother made for you, you can't have them." She

took them for herself when I answered, "I do not want to wear them. Anyone who wants them can have them." Verlie had gone to school only one year and then had married young. She remained a true Traditional all her life, strongly opposing schooling for her own children. My mother said she was glad I was home. If I would stay there, she would not urge me to change my ways. I could wear any kind of clothes that I wanted to wear if I would just stay at home with her.

At this point, Miss Sarah Abbott came into my life. She was the first resident field nurse in Hotevilla, coming there in 1915 from Polacca, where she had served for several years. Miss Abbott was a middle-aged woman, dedicated and kind and understanding. She was slender and had nice features. She had been thrown from a horse in Polacca, resulting in a deep gash which left an ugly scar at the corner of her mouth, which you didn't see, once you knew her. She had learned enough Hopi to be able to converse with the women about their problems. She went about her duties in the village — sometimes on foot and sometimes on horseback — and was a familiar and friendly figure.

She made home visits to the sick (those who would have her), dispensing medicines at the direction of the doctor in Oraibi, sending a messenger for him to come when he was needed, and helping with monthly clinics. She was also responsible for the community laundry and sewing rooms on her premises, where she lived in a cottage. Miss Abbott endeavored to learn and understand the ways and customs of the people. During her visits, if a family should be eating, and if they should invite her to stay and eat with them, she would sit down and eat. She was a good angel in my life from this time until she retired in 1925. When I felt that I just had to get away from the tension in my home, I would go to the sewing room and find relief with Miss Abbott.

During the latter part of October an epidemic of influenza came to Hopi land. So many were stricken that there were not enough well ones to care for the sick. Miss Abbott and myself were among the few in Hotevilla who escaped. Going night and day we did what we could to help the families. She told me what to do. We fixed bottles for the babies, and I went from house to house among my relatives delivering them. I would find cold rooms with no fires and had to chop huge cedar logs into stove size and make a fire. I made big pots of gruel (very thin cornmeal mush) for the patients. There were many deaths.

My older brother was among the first to have the flu. He was up and around, but still weak, when my mother sickened. Then I stayed home to take care of my mother. On the afternoon of the third day of her illness she was very restless. When I spoke to her she did not answer me. She got out of her bed and crawled outside. I tried to make her come back and lie down but she wouldn't, so I let her sit outside in the sun, watching my little brother (Lawrence) play at her side. He climbed into her lap. She didn't say a word. Then I got her back into the house and on her bed and thought she was going to be better.

My father had been out with the sheep that day. He came in at about 4:00 p.m. By sundown, Mother was much worse. I knew that she was dying. We tried to get the medicine man, but there was so much sickness he couldn't come.

My father then began talking to Mother like the medicine man does. He said, "Remember, you are a great person and it is really your own responsibility to get well. If you have the will to get well, it will be so, and you will recover. If you want to live, repent of your sins, put away your sins, think good thoughts, pray with all your might, and you will get well and live." This is psychology, mind over matter, which the Hopis had used long before anyone of them went away to school to hear about psychology.

When you are sick the medicine man asks, "What is wrong with you? What is it that makes your body sick? Think hard, and if you have done or thought wrongly, pray and think until it is no longer in your system, then you will get well." He gives them a little sacred cornmeal and says, "Now you pray on the cornmeal. You pray to get well."

It is a silent prayer from the heart, holding the cornmeal in the hand, with bowed head. Then the medicine man takes the cornmeal to the edge of the village and offers a prayer in behalf of the sick person, leaves the cornmeal there, and God does the rest. Sometimes it is the godfather who does this, in place of the medicine man. Sometimes they do get well for sure; no matter how sick they are, they do get well. But my mother died before my father finished talking to her.

When there is death, all the family leave the house, except two older men who carry out the burial with no delay. I immediately took my little brother by the hand and went to my sister's house. Lawrence kept trying to break away from me, wanting to go back to his mother. I had to use force to make him go with me. We spent the night at Verlie's house. I didn't go back home until after Mother was buried.

Even though my father had come home sick that evening and my brother had barely recovered from the flu, they proceeded with the preperations for the Hopi burial. They washed the body and performed the final hair washing ritual. This ritual is for the purpose of confirming and accepting a person into a clan relationship, as the family unit (clan) is the foundation of Hopi society. This principle apparently transcends mortality, and deceased persons must be reaffirmed into the family before they are buried to insure that they will remain in the family in the "other world." The face is then heavily dusted with cornmeal and covered with a layer of cotton in which holes for eyes and mouth are cut. They put on clothing that was favored by the deceased. Before the body becomes rigid, it is fixed in a sitting position with the knees folded against the chest, the arms around the knees and bound securely with yucca strips. A downy feather is tied to the hair at the top of the head, and another to the ankle, symbolic of the flight of the spirit.

Then the corpse is wrapped in blankets and tied like a bundle with many strips of yucca. My brother, even though he was still weak from the flu, carried the body of his mother on his back about a half mile to the village common burial ground, where he and my father dug the grave in the night. The soil is sandy and easy to dig. They dug a hole about six feet deep and three by six feet length and breadth, then excavated a little room to the side, high enough to contain the corpse, where it was placed. A big slab of sandstone was placed upright to cover the opening, and then the grave was refilled and mounded. The slab is to prevent any wild animal that might dig into the newly dug earth from getting at the body. Rocks were piled over the spot, into which was fixed a greasewood stick about four feet long. This is to provide a way out for the spirit, which leaves the body on the third day. On the third day, a little food and water are taken out and left at the grave that the spirit may partake before it departs for the spirit world.

Upon completing this task, my father and brother went back home. First they carried all the personal belongings, and clothing of the dead, that had been used during the last illness, outside the village where they burned them. Returning to the house they burned cedar branches and pitch on a rock in the rooms to fumigate and purify the house. Next they bathed their bodies in water in which cedar twigs had been boiled, and which had been prepared by one of the women of the family; after putting on clean clothes they were considered cleansed, and the family could now use the house again.

It seemed to take a long time for the flu victims to regain their strength. After performing this strenuous duty, my brother had a relapse; he was in bed for three or four weeks, when he died.

It should have been my place to take over

my mother's household and make a home for my father and my younger brothers, since I was unmarried and living at home. I should have inherited my mother's house. But my sister brought her big family of children and her husband and moved right in. Mother's house was bigger than Verlie's. This placed me in an awkward position, a sort of outsider with no place nor part in the family. My younger brother said, "I don't see why they have to move in on us. You can cook and take care of us and make a home for us and we would like it better."

I could do nothing that would please my sister, Verlie. Even though I carried the water from the spring myself, she would get after me for using so much water for bathing and washing my clothes, which I felt I had to do to keep clean. Even when I read, it irritated her. She nagged and nagged at me all the time. When I had done my daily share of chores I would slip away and go to the community laundry and sewing room and spend the day with Miss Abbott.

Appliances in the laundry room consisted of a wood stove, water on tap, and round, galvanized tubs with old-fashioned washboards and benches and irons to be heated on the stove; we had to heat the water on the stoves too. There would be other girls there. After I had washed my clothes I would take a bath and wash my hair in the same round tub.

When the flu epidemic became bad in Phoenix (1918-1919) Emory decided to go home for a while. He expected to go back to his job and more school in Phoenix. He stopped and was working in Winslow when word came to him that his people were all sick with the flu, so he came on home to Bacabi to help. He had been home for more than a month before he came to see me because it was such a sad time with so much sickness and death in every village. Emory's godfather (Susie's husband) died about the same time that my mother did. Every family was in sorrow. Boys do not visit their girl friends when they are in mourning, but Emory would write a note and bring it at night and slip it in a crack by the door where I would find it in the morning. I remember one said, "I am very sorry that your mother died and I sympathize with you. As soon as we are out of sorrow here for a little while, I will come and see you."

When Emory did come over he could see for himself my situation. The experiences we had just passed through had matured us both. He proposed that we get married. He said he was not in a position to support me too well, yet; but we were rich in love. He had a job at the government school at Hotevilla in charge of the buildings and the power plant, and it looked good to me.

Marriage

THE HOME OF THE bridegroom is the center of activity in a Hopi wedding. When a couple decides to marry, the father of the groom takes over. He furnishes everything — cotton for the weaving and food to feed the workers during the time the weaving is in progress. Each household keeps a supply of cotton on hand against the time when a son may marry.

In Emory's case there was a problem. His parents had separated years before and his

mother had remarried and lived in Oraibi.
Emory lived with his mother during his childhood; Wickvaya, Emory's grandfather, also
lived in the same household. This is why Wickvaya took his grandson to school at Keams Canyon and brought him back in the spring.
Emory's father was among the men sent to the
Indian School at Carlisle in Pennsylvania for
five years, in 1906. When he returned he went
to Hotevilla to live, and in due time remarried.
Emory had never lived with his father.

Emory's mother wanted us to come to her
home in Oraibi, but Emory had been away at
school so many years that it wasn't really home
to him. As he grew older he had lived in Bacabi,
with his cousin Susie and her husband, who was
his godfather, during the summers that he was
home, helping in whatever way he could. Susie
invited us to come to her home, and Emory's
uncles and cousins all helped put in for the cotton and food and were the hosts for us.

After we decided to get married, I spent
every minute that I could grinding in preparation for feeding the wedding guests. Women
and girls of my relatives who wanted to help
started grinding too. When my sister Verlie
walked with me to Bacabi to Susie's house, I carried a big pan full of fine white cornmeal. I
never left Susie's house for the entire period
(about a month) and was under her watchful

care, even slept with her the first three nights.

As a bride I was considered sacred the first few days, being in a room with the shades on the windows, talking to no one. All this time I was steadily grinding corn which was brought in by Emory's kinswomen. Each brought, say, a quart of corn in a basket or on a plaque to be passed in to me to be ground, each lot separately. After the first grinding I handed the corn out and waited while it was roasted and passed back to me to be ground real fine. As each lot was finished, I put it back into its own container, lining it up along the wall with others. When the aunts came back in the evening to get their corn there was food on the table and they ate. White corn was the grist the first day, blue corn on the second and third days. At the end of each day Susie gave me a relaxing rubdown.

Early each morning of the first three days, Cousin Susie went with me to the east edge of the mesa, and there, facing the rising sun, we bowed our heads and each offered a silent prayer for a happy married life. Our days began with the rising of the sun and ended with its setting, because there was no artificial light for night working.

The fourth day is the actual wedding day. Everyone of the relatives is up when the cock crows, to participate in the marriage ritual, the hair washing. Suds are made from the tuber of

the yucca root, pounded into a pulp, put into two
basins of water, and worked with the hands
until the pan is filled with foamy suds.

Two pans were placed side by side on the
floor, where Susie and my sister Verlie prepared
the suds. Usually the mothers of the bride and
groom do this. Susie and Verlie acted for our
mothers. While Susie washed my hair, Verlie
washed Emory's. Then each took a strand of hair
and twisted them together hard and tight as a
symbol of acceptance of the new in-law into the
clan (family) and also to bind the marriage
contract, as they said, "Now you are united,
never to go apart."

Next Emory was taken outside and stripped
to the waist by the women of my family. Each
had brought her small container of water which
she poured over his shoulders as he knelt over
a tub. They splashed the water over him with
their hands. It was still dark, so they could not
see him; they put a blanket around him, and
he came back into the house to get warm from
that icy bath.

Now, with our hair still wet and hanging
loose, Emory and I walked together to the eastern edge of the village and once more faced the
rising sun, and with bowed heads we prayed in
silence for a long time; for a good life together,
for children, and to be together all of our lives
and never stray from each other.

After my hair was dry on this day, they combed it up like a married woman, never to be worn in maiden style again. Married women parted their hair from the center in the front to the nape of the neck. Each side was folded over the hand until it reached nearly to the ear where it was bound with a cord made from hair and a little yarn, leaving a soft puff at the ends. The hair in front of the ears was cut into side-burns about two inches long.

The making of the robes begins on the morning of the nuptial hair washing. The father or uncle of the groom (in our case Susie's father) took a bag of cotton and, passing through the village, stopped at each house. He was expected, and each housewife opened her door and extended a plaque to receive some cotton (everyone was required to wash his hands before touching the cotton). Immediately all hands went to work cleaning the cotton of seeds, burrs, and little sticks. It was all cleaned that same day.

In the evening the uncles, godfather, and men who wished to help, gathered at the groom's house to card the cotton. The cards were a pair 'of flat, wire-toothed brushes, four by twelve inches, with wooden handles at a slight angle, on the long side. They were bought from the trader and used for both wool and cotton. I watched my father and my grandfather use them in my time. A small handful of cotton was spread over all the teeth of one card; with the second card, the cotton was combed back and forth until all the lumps were out and it became fluffy. Another motion made it into a strip as long as the card, which strip was put aside and another one started. The men worked late carding big piles of white cotton. Coal-oil lamps lighted their work. During this time the men told stories, with the bride sitting nearby, along with the kinswomen. From time to time the bride thanked the workers for their service. Everyone enjoyed the stories, and before they realized it, it was midnight and quitting time. The men were served refreshments and everyone went home to bed. It took several nights to do the carding.

All the men in the village worked to spin this cotton into thread in one day. Food was obtained and prepared to feed the whole village. Ten or fifteen sheep were required. If the host didn't have sheep of his own, he bought them. One or two might be donated by someone. Wood had to be brought in for the cooking and to heat the kivas.

At sunrise on spinning day the custodian of each kiva went early to clean up his kiva and start the fire and get it warm. The women were busy too, putting the big kettles on the fire and adding ingredients for the stew, making ready every plaque and basket.

After his breakfast, each man went to his kiva, taking his spindle (every adult male owns one). Emory's uncle came around early to deliver to each kiva the carded cotton to be spun. In Bacabi there were three kivas. Soon all spindles were humming away. Emory's uncle checked the kivas from time to time to keep them all supplied with carded cotton. Dinner would be late, so they were served a snack at noon in the kiva. The spun cotton was made into skeins; the warp thread was finer than the woof. The pile of light, fluffy hanks of warp and woof thread was beautiful.

In the meantime the women were getting the food and tables ready. My relatives and myself were served earlier so we could be free to serve the community dinner. However, the bride did not serve but mingled with the other women. They teased me as all made merry and had a happy time. The men were served at the tables in Susie's house and neighboring houses as needed, and then the women and children of the village ate. Whatever food was left, especially the stew, was divided among the people.

The weaving took about two weeks, and it began a few days after the spinning was finished. One sheep was butchered this time, and the other foods were made ready for the first day of the weaving. At dawn and before breakfast the three special looms used in wedding weaving were brought out from their storage place to the kiva (one kiva) where they were untied and spread out on the floor. Two or three men at a time worked at the long and tedious job of stringing each loom, rolling the warp back and forth to each other, over the notches close together on the two end poles.

The bridal clothing consisted of a robe six by eight feet, a second one about four by six feet to cover the shoulders, and a girdle about ten inches wide and eight feet long, which is tied around the waist. The moccasins had leggings made of white buckskin. Then there is the reed roll, which is a sort of suitcase in which to wrap and carry extra gifts. Emory gathered the reeds from the edge of the wash, cut them into uniform lengths and tied them together with cord like a bamboo window blind.

The threaded looms were hung from loops in the ceiling beams and fastened to loops on the floor and stretched tight, and the weaving began, the best weavers taking turns during the day. The belt is braided rather than woven.

At noon, food was brought to the kiva by relatives. After dinner a man took his place at each loom and worked until evening. The host did not weave all the time, but he stayed with them at all times. In the evening each man carried the loom he had worked on to Susie's house, where I received them and put them away in a back room for safekeeping. The men sat down to eat of piki and beans and leftover food from dinner and somviki, which is tamales made from finely ground blue corn, sweetened and wrapped in corn husks, and tied with yucca strips and then boiled, and made by the bride every evening. As the weavers left after supper, I gave each of them a few tamales on top of a folded piki. Each morning the weaving continued. Only one man could work on each loom at a time, but the best weavers came and took turns during the day. Other men came, bringing their spinning or knitting, or just sat and visited and listened as the older men retold the traditional stories. Sometimes they all sang together.

About halfway through the rites, our consciences troubled us, because we felt the Hopi way was not quite right. We decided to get a license and be married legally. Emory told his folks what we wanted to do. He made application to the agency at Keams Canyon, and a marriage license was obtained by mail from Holbrook, the nearest county seat. It took about a week. In the afternoon that the license came, I went to my father's house in Hotevilla; Emory went with me. I just walked in and told my father that I was going to be married by license that night and had come to get my clothes. I could feel the disapproval of my father and my sister as I gathered the things I was going to wear. I just could not stay there and get dressed. I took my clothes and went to one of the school teachers, and she let me dress in her house.

I was married in a white batiste dress, which was my pride and joy. I had earned the money and bought the material and made the dress in domestic art class in the Phoenix school. It had lace insertion set in bow knots around the gathered skirt, on the flared sleeves, and on the collar. My teacher had entered it in the State Fair, and I got second prize on it. I wore it once to a party and then decided it was too nice to wear and put it away in a box.

Later I made this dress into two little dresses for my first baby, our little girl "Joy." About the second time that I hung these dresses out on the clothesline to dry, one of them disappeared. Two years later I was getting water at the spring one day, and there was a little two-year-old girl playing around, wearing that dress. I took her by the hand, led her to my house, and took off the dress (it was too little for her anyway). I put a nice colorful gingham dress on her, and gave her some bread and jam. She was pleased with it all, as I opened the door and sent her home. I heard no more on that. My babies wore out those dresses.

We were married in the evening on February 14, 1919, in the living room of the home of Mr. Anderson, principal of the school in Hotevilla, by Reverend Dirkson of the Mennonite Mission. Emory's people, including some of his cousins, came to the ceremony. The teachers served some refreshments and gave us some little presents and a room where we could spend the night. In the morning they served a wedding breakfast, and then we went back to finish the tribal wedding rites at Bacabi.

Emory was working at the school and had to be on the job, so he wasn't able to participate in the weaving during the daytime. The activity died down after the first few days anyway, the weavers carrying on until everything was done. I helped with the grinding and cooking until the outfit was completed.

When the weaving was finished the men took the robes from the looms and brought them into the house to be tried on. A border of sixteen running stitches in red was embroidered in the two corners, suggesting a limit of sixteen children, the most a person should have, and four stitches in each of the other two corners in orange, suggesting a minimum number of children. The white moccasins with leggings in one piece were finished just in time to be put on with the rest of the outfit. It was by then evening; food was placed before the guests and everyone ate again. (Hopis do not invite you to eat. They set the food before you, and the food invites.)

The next morning before sunup, Susie led the others in clothing me, first washing my hair. Everyone admired the bride, and I was now ready to go back to my father's house. A line of white cornmeal was sprinkled on the ground, pointing the way. There was a lot of snow on the ground, so they wrapped rags over my white moccasins so I wouldn't get them wet or muddy. Emory's people went with me out of the village and over the little hill back to my home in Hotevilla. Emory did not go with me this time. How I wished that my own dear mother could be there to meet me. The sun was just coming up when we got to my father's house. Verlie opened the door, and my father thanked them for the beautiful bridal apparel that would make his daughter eligible to enter the world of the hereafter. Thus ends the wedding ritual.

I went inside and removed the wedding apparel and spread it out on the bed. Then all the clan women came in and admired and tried on the robes. Then everything was rolled up and stored away. After a period of time these may be used as needed, even cut into kilts for men to wear or to make bags to carry packs on burros.

A bride of the village who has been married in the preceding year should dress in her complete bridal attire and go into the plaza at the time of the Home Dance, accompanied by her mother-in-law, and show herself to the kachinas during their last round of the day, thus establishing her status as a married woman in their eyes. We had gone to Idaho but were back by the Home Dance in July. My father had shown his disapproval of me by cutting up my big robe and making little kilts out of it. I had taken the small robe with me. I had my moccasins and did make this appearance, accompanied by Susie.

Miss Abbott came to see me once during the thirty days of the tribal ceremony. She said she did not want to embarrass me, but she whispered in my ear, "You have never looked better in your life. You look healthy and happy. You have rosy cheeks. This has done you good."

The groom may follow the bride to her home as soon as he likes. Some go right away, some wait a long time before claiming their brides. Emory came over after a few days and stayed a couple of nights, but I could see that the tension and hostility was hard on him; too many children, too little room, not even a room to ourselves. After my going through all that ceremony just to please my family, my sister was still so hostile that I felt neither wanted nor welcome.

One day, about a month after we were married, when no one was at home, I felt that I could not stand it another minute. I gathered and packed my belongings, as many as I could carry, returning later for the rest of them, and went to the house where Emory lived near the school. He was at his work teaching shop when I got there. I cleaned up the house and had a meal cooked when he came home, and we were real happy. Soon afterward I got a job teaching beginners in the school. It was hard to get teachers there because it was so isolated.

Idaho, Here We Come

WHEN THE SCHOOL YEAR ended in the spring of 1919, we left Hotevilla, and went to Lapwai, Idaho, the center for the Nez Perce Indian tribe. Dr. Breid, whom we had known in Keams Canyon, had been transferred there. He wrote asking us to come and work in the school and the tuberculosis sanitarium. We decided to accept this offer. Emory asked his brother John to take us to Winslow. We loaded our things into the wagon. A young Hopi girl named Olive traveled with us. She was going to work in the home of Dr. Breid. We camped one night and were in Winslow the next evening.

We went by train from Winslow, through Bakersfield and Stockton in California, where we changed cars and went on to Sacramento. We had never been away from the southwestern deserts, and the sight of the big trees and streams of water and green grass was wonderful. The conductor always made a little speech about the sights before we came to them so that we knew what we were seeing. The train stopped to take on water at a mineral spring. The water looked so good that we all took out our folding cups to take a drink, but the minerals were so strong that the water didn't taste good. But it was a beautiful spring.

We rode past Mt. Shasta and other peaks and wound up a mountainside and into a tunnel. The tunnel was long and the cars filled up with smoke from the engines.

Early the next morning we passed into Oregon's virgin forests where the grass was green and thick and there were hundreds upon hundreds of sheep. We always had little flocks of sheep. I had never seen so many sheep in my life. We went on past Salem, Oregon, where there was a school for Indians near the railroad. Here the landscape and houses looked like Phoenix. On to Portland, Oregon, where on one side of the Columbia River is Oregon and on the other side is Washington. There we were to change cars again. We went into a big depot for a two-hour wait. I had never before seen such a big place. The room was as big as an auditorium, with rest rooms, nursery, library, and restaurant, and announcers calling the arrival and departure of trains. This was all new to me.

We wanted to see things, and I needed something to keep me warm. Even though it was spring, it got cold. We started out. The street was crooked and narrow like an old town. We soon got to the skyscrapers. The streets were so crowded with people, there was a policeman working hard at each corner to get them across. We started to go, but each time they let the crowd pass, we only took one step, and then another crowd moved ahead of us. When we got to the other end of the block, we decided to go back, for fear there wouldn't be time. I was so interested in the buildings that I kept looking up at them, and more than once I lost Emory. They must have been apartment houses. There was laundry hanging and it looked like handkerchiefs fluttering in the wind, but it must have been sheets. We stopped at a little store and bought a sweater for me and finally got back to the depot.

We left there in the afternoon and in a short

time it was dark and we couldn't see things any-
more. Next morning we passed through Pendle-
ton, Oregon, and on to Lewiston, Idaho, which
is on the Snake River. There we changed cars
again, and it was only seven miles to Lapwai.
This was a little, narrow-gauge train, and it
looked like a toy. We crossed the Snake River,
which joins the Columbia River with a big roar-
ing noise just a little way from Lapwai. The cars
were ferried across to the town of Lapwai.

Dr. Breid met us, but even though they
knew we were coming they didn't have a place
ready for us. They put two beds in the corner
of a big room where we could live for a few days.
It didn't seem very much like home, and I wondered why we thought we wanted to come.
Emory had a job as an engineer in the power
plant, and he started to work right off, but I had
no job for a while. In about ten days the man
whom Emory replaced, left, and we moved into
the house he vacated. It had taken all the money
we had saved to pay for the railroad tickets, and
we were hard put to eat until the first paycheck.
Since we were too proud to borrow, we got along
as best we could. One day in the mail was a government envelope addressed to me. I was anxious to get it open. It was a check for nine dollars, a bonus on my teaching salary in Hotevilla,
a godsend, which tided us over and for which
we were truly happy.

Each employee was given a piece of land for a garden, if he had a family and wanted to grow vegetables. The man before us had planted a garden. We would work in the garden after working hours. We raised tomatoes, potatoes, pumpkins, and other vegetables. There were blackberries everywhere, and you could have the berries that bordered you. In a few months our Dr. Breid was transferred, and we bought a flock of chickens from him. We had more eggs than we could use. I saved them up and traded them for groceries at the store, where they were glad to get fresh eggs.

We harvested five hundred pounds of potatoes. Since we could not use all of them we took two hundred pounds to the cellar in the sanitarium; the others we sacked and stored under the house. Neighbors had told us how cold it would get. We kept some potatoes in the room to use, put by the wall with the kitchen stove on the other side. It was such a severe winter that our potatoes turned to rocks, and we lost them all. We bought potatoes from the store in small quantities. We moved our bed into our front room and kept lots of coal in our big heater when we went to bed, but by morning we would have frost on our hair from breathing.

The school had a big orchard of apples, peaches, and plums. The employees were free to take as much as they wanted. We got our share. We had a surplus of tomatoes from our garden, which I canned after working hours. Everybody seemed to have plenty of everything.

The cook at the club house (where the unmarried employees lived) left soon after we got settled. They hired me when I told them I could cook. I cooked for twenty people all the time, with visitors often making it up to twenty-five, and I had no help. I had to do everything, wait table, wash dishes, bake bread, and do the cleaning. It was a pretty hard job for me. I complained a little, so a patient was sent over from the sanitarium to help me. She was able to wait tables but nothing else. I still had too much to do. I worked myself sick and said I was going to quit. They offered to raise my pay. I was getting thirty-five dollars a month. They liked my cooking and hated to see me leave, but I did.

Then I was offered a government job as assistant cook in the sanitarium kitchen. There was a head cook and three assistants, and it was easier. The pay was sixty-five dollars monthly.

Next I transferred to the sewing room, where a seamstress was needed, and where the pay was seventy dollars a month. The head seamstress cut out things and I did the sewing. I made about fifty dresses for girls — all alike — uniforms. Some of the girls (patients) went to school when they were able, and they wore the uniforms to church on Sunday.

I had expected to find things with Indians up there different — somehow, better — but they were just like other Indians. They had good fertile land but did not work it themselves, leasing it out to white men. The lease money was paid through the agency, and every month we would see lots of long-haired, blanketed Indians, hanging around waiting to get their lease money. They didn't work at anything. Just like Navajo men, they spent their time loafing in the streets and other places. A few lived in fine houses and drove Cadillacs with their long hair in a knot and a blanket over their shoulders, while the rest lived in hovels.

We stayed in Lapwai until the end of the school year and would have liked to stay longer. The superintendent wanted us to stay, but Olive got sick, even before school was out. She was frail when she came. She wanted to go back to Hotevilla and was really not able to travel alone, so we felt we had to take her.

We had been able to save our money so that when we had to go we were prepared. Since Olive did not have enough money to pay all of her fare home, we paid ours and part of hers. Back to Hotevilla we went.

Olive died in about two months.

Hotevilla

WHEN WE CAME BACK from Idaho in May,
1920, we stayed with Susie in Bacabi until my
house in Hotevilla was vacated. I had fallen heir
to my sister's house when she took over my
mother's house there in Hotevilla. We cleaned
the house and made it as nice as we could.
Emory went right to work planting a field of
corn, twelve miles out from the village. Life was
good for Emory and me. There was love and
understanding in our home, and we were

expecting. In a short time my two younger brothers, Henry and Lawrence, ages sixteen and eight, respectively, came to live with us and were a part of our family until they married — and they still are.

The spring that burst out of the sandrock cliffs at the edge of the village furnished plenty of water. For household use it was dipped from a rock-enclosed basin and carried up a steep trail to the homes in the village. The surplus water ran into a larger basin and was used to irrigate small, terraced garden spots. Each family had its own plot. When the water was low, the women dipped it out into a ditch so it would run onto their gardens. When the water was high, it would run out. We raised chilis, beans, tomatoes, squash, onions, and a little corn. Peach trees, introduced by the Spaniards, grew among the cedar trees near the village. The big cornfields were farther out in the valley where the soil was rich and water was furnished by the summer floods.

Emory bought a wagon and four horses with the money that we had saved from our Idaho venture and started freighting supplies for the Lorenzo Hubbell Trading Post at Oraibi, from the railroad points at Winslow and Flagstaff. Everyone who had a freight outfit had his turn at hauling. It took about a week to make the round trip. Sometimes when a government employee was moving out there would be a pay-load outbound, hauling out his things; also when the sheep were sheared in the spring, the wagons were loaded with the big sacks of wool as they went to the railroad. An advantage of this was that Emory could buy for us at the railroad ware-houses; the prices on the Reservation were greatly increased, due to the transportation costs. He got flour for two dollars for a hundred pounds. Emory made a trip about once a month, sometimes oftener, so we had some cash. He still had time to farm and raise corn near Hote-villa.

The freighters made and maintained the roads themselves. When a stretch was too steep or rocky or sandy, they would take time to work it enough to make it passable. It was about the same distance to Winslow and Flagstaff, but Winslow was the usual destination.

Emory recalls some freighting experiences:

We used one wagon and four horses and would travel two or more outfits, sometimes as many as ten going together, because if we got stuck we needed help and company. It took two days out with an empty wagon but longer if we had a load. We camped in the town campyard. It took one to two days to load; we helped each other load the freight. We would get an early start on the return trip which usually took three

*days. Winter or summer the freight must go
through; the trader must have his merchandise.
The journey was safe as a rule but in stormy
weather one must be alert for danger.*

*We had to cross the Little Colorado River.
The best crossing was at Leupp or Black Falls
near Wupatki. The crossing was not bad except
when the river was in flood from summer rains
or spring thaws. There were potholes in the
sandstone river bottom. One would be obliged
to walk barefooted with pants removed through
the icy cold water to scout out the course for the
wagon and team. One time one of my lead horses
slipped into a deep hole with his hind leg, but
the other horses dragged him out so that the
wagon missed the hole and didn't tip over.*

*We used greasewood for our camp fires.
When burned down to coals, it holds the heat
for a long time. After cooking supper, especially
in winter, freighters might just sit by the fire,
talking and talking, keeping warm rather than
going to a cold bed.*

*Once I made a trip with some older freight-
ers. The first night out we younger ones were
so tired that we rolled out our beds near the fire
and got into them as soon as we had eaten, and
listened as the older men sat and talked. Finally
they felt hungry again, so they got out the frying pan and broke up some piki into it, added
a little salt and lard and heated it over the coals,*

*shaking it all the time; then setting it aside to
cool a little. I reached out and got a handful and
ate it, and another and another, until the piki
was all gone. The men were so interested in
their conversation that they forgot about their
piki. One, finding the pan empty and thinking
the others had eaten the piki, heated a second
panful and again set it aside to cool, and again
the men talked while we boys ate the piki. The
third time round they discovered where their
piki had gone.*

*I freighted off and on until the Ford trucks
began taking over the hauling and the freight
team and wagon had to go. I then spent all of
my time taking care of my crops and sheep.*

In due time my first baby, a little girl, was
born. We named her Joy, and she opened the
door of joy that a baby brings to its parents,
"out of God's wondrous ways." When a birth
is imminent, all the Hopi family leave the house,
and the prospective mother is left with a male
relative as her helper. I had an older cousin who
was very good and I liked him. He helped me
with my first baby. Later on Emory got to be
quite an expert, and we were alone most of the
time when I had the other nine of my ten children. I was all alone twice.

A place is prepared in a corner of the room,
a sheepskin on the floor with some clean soft

cloth and a chair or stool to rest on, near the stove if it is in winter. When a pain comes on, the mother goes to this place and sits in a squatting position or on her knees during the duration of the pain. Her helper is behind her with his arms around her body, high, giving support to her back as she leans against him. She folds her arms across her body and they both exert mild downward pressure. She is exhorted, "Don't open your mouth to yell or cry or scream and let the air out. Keep the air in to help expel the baby." Between pains the mother may walk about the room or sit as she feels like doing. But some women do make a lot of noise, screaming and crying all the time. No one is to touch the woman internally.

When the baby comes the mother takes a good rest, leaning against her helper. Then they go to work to get the afterbirth. She takes a deep breath and presses on the stomach a little. This helps to get the body back in shape as well as to expel the afterbirth. The cord is not cut until the placenta is expelled. So it is a joint project of labor for both the man and woman to deliver the baby. The mother is now given some cedar water with which she gives herself a sponge bath.

Sand that has been heated in the oven or before the fireplace is spread between cloths and placed over the sheepskin, and the spent mother rests upon it. The sand acts as a blotter and the heat relaxes. Hot rocks are placed at the feet and near the legs, and the mother is covered well, and she has a well-earned rest.

The midwife is called to take care of the baby. She cuts the cord and ties it with hair from the mother's head. (I took care of some of my babies, Emory handing me things.) Then she uses a little warm water and cleans the baby. While the new little body is still damp she sprinkles it well all over with a special kind of ashes, "baby ashes," soft like baby powder. These ashes are found at the foot of Blue Point, south of Oraibi, called Baby Ashes Mountain, where there used to be a volcano. Under the top layer there is this very fine gray, powdery ash, of which a good supply is obtained ahead of time by the father. This makes the skin very soft and clean and will keep the hair from growing on the skin too much. This ash treatment is repeated every day for twenty days.

After the birth of her child, the mother stays in bed for three days, and she fasts for nineteen days — that is, she eats no salt or meat, just corn and well-cooked vegetables. She does not carry water or chop wood. All this care and attention makes the young mother feel loved and cherished.

The mother-in-law will come in every day for a period of twenty days, to care for her son's wife, if she lives in the same village. But if she lives in another village she comes in every fourth day. When she first comes she brings two ears of corn, perfect ones with kernels all the way to the tip; a long one represents the mother, and a little one represents the baby. These two ears of corn are put in the bed beside the baby for the twenty days, symbolic of mother nature.

On the first day the mother-in-law draws on each of the four walls of the room, with white corn meal, five horizontal lines, each six inches long, to tell off the twenty days. She brings water enough for the day. Then she bathes the baby and rubs the wet little body with baby ashes and wraps it in a blanket. The mother's hair is washed, and she is given a steam bath. Cedar twigs are placed in a wash basin and covered with water. A good-sized, heated rock is put on the twigs. The mother stands over the pan with legs on each side of it. A thick blanket is draped over her to form a tent. The heat from the rock fills the tent with steam which penetrates the body. As one rock cools another hot one is added until four rocks are used. It really makes you feel good. Every fourth day one line is rubbed off each wall. If the mother-in-law is from another village a midwife or a sister will care for the mother on the days she does not come in. Since Emory's mother lived in Oraibi, she came every fourth day.

On the twentieth day, the birth ritual is climaxed with the naming of the baby and a feast. The female relatives come early, while it is still dark, each bringing a small container of water which she pours into a basin. The mother is bathed and her hair washed. Grandmother works up a soapweed lather, holds the baby, and washes its hair, as a symbol that the newborn is accepted into the family. Each aunt in turn dips her hand into the water and rubs her dampened hand over the little baby head. White cornmeal is rubbed on the baby face, and the body is bathed. Now, Grandmother wraps the baby in a blanket, and the group sits on the floor in a circle, while Grandmother cradles the baby in her left arm. In her right hand she takes the two perfect ears of corn (the mother and the baby one) and passes them back and forth over the little body as she makes her wish or blessing as follows:

"You shall live to be a very old man (or woman). You shall have no sickness during your lifetime. You shall have all the blessings that can be had and enjoy life as you go along. You shall die without sickness, just go to sleep. You shall bear the name of . . . ." Here she gives the name she wants the child to be called. She puts a little pinch of white cornmeal in the baby's mouth and says, "This is your food, which the earth mother will give you all your life."

Having finished her blessing, the grandmother passes the infant to the aunt sitting beside her; the aunt repeats her blessing and suggests a name for the baby. Only those who wish to give a name participate. The mother and the grandmother must remember all of the names as they go together, carrying the infant to the eastern edge of the mesa, where, facing the rising sun, they implore him to take cognizance of this little Hopi baby whose name is to be . . . (repeating the six or so names that have been suggested) and to bless this child with all good gifts of life. Later the parents chose one name, and the child is known by it.

When the mother and grandmother come back from the Sun Prayer, a feast is spread and everyone partakes of piki, mutton stew, and pudding, which has been prepared and brought in by the relatives. Some of the surplus food is presented to the grandmother in payment for her services, which are now completed; however she may carry water longer if she wants to do so. On the two days preceeding the Naming, the aunts fill all the water jars so the new mother will not have to go to the spring for water for several days.

When our baby was about a week old I wrapped her in a blanket and put her on a cradleboard and handled her as little as possible. Emory's mother wove my first cradleboard, but Emory made the others from a board. My babies were all put on the cradleboard. It keeps them warm and makes them easy to handle. I had to do my work so I trained them not to cry too much by just letting them cry it out at first. When the baby cried, I would put the cradle-board on my back and go ahead with my work. If I were grinding corn the motion would soothe him and he would feel close to me and be comforted. After a while he would go to sleep and I would put him down.

The new mother is isolated from her husband for forty days after the first baby comes; twenty-five for succeeding births. I nursed all of my babies until they were a year old. This and the forty days of isolation were to make sure that the babies don't come too close together. When my babies were six to eight months old I started feeding them a little food from the table.

I had the first real store-bought diapers and soft little blankets and safety pins in Hotevilla. Very often, after I had washed them, some diapers or maybe a blanket would be missing from the clothesline.

Our little Joy died of dysentery when she was about a year old. I didn't see her after she was dead. They wanted to spare me, so they just went ahead as soon as possible preparing her for burial. We all left the house except Emory and my father, who proceeded to wash the body and clothe it in her prettiest dress. They rubbed her face with white cornmeal and tied a downy feather to her hair (symbol of purity and flight of the spirit). After wrapping the body in blankets and tying it into a bundle, they carried it out of the village.

If a baby is stillborn, or if it dies before the naming ceremony is finished on the twentieth day of its life, the paternal grandmother will then wash the baby's hair and also give it a name by which it will be known in the hereafter. After that, the parents will proceed with the burial.

Infants are not buried but are placed in a crevice high among the rocks quite a distance from the village. The men bow their heads and pray: "God, please take this sweet little spirit and let her share this resting place with you for a little while, and then let her return to earth again." If a family loses more than one infant, both are placed in the same crevice, the first one being removed and the newly dead corpse being placed on the bottom and the first one replaced on the top. The usual rites of purification of the house and of the male participants are performed.

In due time, we had our second baby, a boy, and we named him "Wayne." When Wayne was six months old he was quite sick. There was a hospital in Keams Canyon, which had been open for a short time. I wanted to take my baby there. My sister opposed it, but the field nurse urged me to go, even took me there in a car. Our baby was in the hospital for about six months. I am sure that he would have died had he not had this hospital care.

Emory was working at Keams Canyon at this time on the construction of government buildings. He had been coming home for week-ends. Since the hospital was new and quite empty, they let Emory and me have one of the rooms. Most of the Indians were afraid of the hospital and wouldn't bring in their sick. Navajos will not go near a dead body or a place where one has died. This presented a problem, and the doctors learned to keep some things secret.

Living in Hotevilla was just like living in any little country town where everyone sees and knows and talks about what everyone else does, only more so. The keynote was "conform," and one who failed to do so felt the lash of disapproval. Our lives were a combination of what we thought was the good of both cultures, the Hopi way and what we had learned at school. Whenever we departed from the traditions, our neighbors would scorn us. They were greatly offended because we were friendly with the government workers, the teachers, and the nurses, and even let them come into our house. When

I washed my clothes and hung them out to dry or worked in my little garden plot, I could feel critical eyes following my every move. When I went to the spring for water, nearly every time I would meet a woman on the trail or at the spring who would bawl me out about something; even the clothes I wore on my back were taboo. I didn't wear the traditional dress. I did not enter wholeheartedly into all of the community social and religious events. Good traditional Hopi women sit all day in the plaza, maybe several days at a time, watching the dances. They have so many that I begrudged the time. I would rather stay home and care for my house, or read, which I often did. I was aware that my neighbors were talking about me, laughing at me, mimicking, and generally belittling me all the time.

There were others besides Emory who had horses, and Navajo horses were loose around too. The fields were not fenced, and if horses ate the corn, Emory's horses were always blamed. If a man came to bawl out Emory when he was not there, the man would take it out on me. In spite of this atmosphere we went about our daily tasks content in our own hearts about the way we did things.

Months passed, years came and went, bringing their cycles of work and joy and pain. We had more babies, about three years apart.

After Wayne, there were four more sons —
Eugene, Emory, Abbott, and LeRoy, growing
up with the village boys. Then came a daughter
Allison and another son Selwyn, who died when
he was a year old; he got up in the night and
bumped his head on the sewing machine so hard
that he died about a month later from the effects
of it. There was another daughter, Marlene. All
were born while we lived in Hotevilla. We added
more rooms to make the house big enough for
all of us. We had a good family life. Our children went to the day school and learned from
nature and each other. Our son Edward, the last
one, was born after we moved out to the ranch.

We worked hard, like Hopis are supposed
to do, and were self-sustaining even during the
Depression, when there were no jobs and no
money. At that time corn brought one cent for a
pound, and we sold it only to buy the things we
couldn't raise. It took a twenty-five pound bag
of shelled corn to buy two spools of thread or
a half-gallon of kerosene for our one lamp. I
used to gather yucca roots and use them for suds
for my washing as well as for shampoo.

While my neighbors were buying white
flour and later bread at the store, I ground the
corn for our bread on the stone mata and matake.
(Later we bought a little hand mill that I screw
on the kitchen table.)

Every year we stored all the food that we

could raise. Hopis had only one way of preserv-
ing food — they dried everything — peaches
cut in half, even squash and melons cut in strips,
were dried in the sun on the flat housetops or on
the big sandrocks near the village. I canned and
bottled the fruit and vegetables as I had learned
to do at school. Only when I ran out of bottles
did I dry my produce.

Ways of preparing corn for the table are
many and varied. I made hominy, using ashes
from the greasewood fire to eat off the hulls.
The dry corn is boiled for an hour or so in the
water with the ashes. The water is drained away
and the corn washed many times, after which it
is boiled a long time until it is tender. A mutton
bone added to the pot gives a fine flavor.

I mixed blue cornmeal with water, rolled it
into balls the size of a walnut, and dropped them
in boiling water to cook and be eaten with milk
as a breakfast cereal. Sometimes I ground dried
peaches or dried meat and mixed them with the
cornmeal for variety. I kept parched corn on
hand for the children if they were hungry
between meals.

Once when I was making jelly, the old-fashioned way where you boil it a long time, I put
a little jelly in a saucer and set it in a low window
to cool and see if it would jell. The screen on the
window had a little hole in it. I had to tend to
my boiling, and when I thought the jelly would

be cool I went to get it. There was nothing in the saucer. I didn't know what had happened to my jelly as no one was around, so I put some more out to cool and watched. Pretty soon a dirty little hand came through the screen and a finger dipped up the jelly and the hand pulled back. I ran around the house, quick. It was Wayne, five years old. When there was a community dinner, I enjoyed seeing the people relish my canned peaches and jelly.

The Department of Health held a clinic in the village every week. I took my children there for prevention shots for smallpox, diphtheria, and whooping cough. One nurse said to me, "I wish all the patients were like your children; they are easy to work with." When the children got sick, I did what I could for them. If they didn't get better I called the nurse or the doctor. Most people called the medicine man and wouldn't let the doctor touch their children.

I always checked with the visiting nurse every month when I was pregnant. However, the hospital was in Keams Canyon, thirty-six miles away, and as our transportation was by horse and wagon, and with my family of little children, we just couldn't get to the hospital. So I had all of my babies like my mother and the mothers for generations before me had theirs — at home.

I did my sewing at the government-spon-

sored sewing room until Emory bought me my
first sewing machine, a Singer treadle in 1934,
while he was still freighting for Mr. Hubbell.
It took the money from two or three trips to pay
for it. After that I sewed for some of the government employees. One certain nurse, Edna
Hill, hired me to make all of her uniforms of
navy blue cotton. She had a queer stout figure
which no store-bought pattern would fit. I made
a pattern that fit her perfectly. We worked
together a good deal.

When my good friend Sarah Abbott retired
and left Hotevilla she took a picture of me that
I had had enlarged and tinted while I was in
Phoenix. She said, "When I am ready to die I
will send it back to you. When you get this picture back, you will know that I am dead." I
have never received the portrait, and now I think
I never shall.

In 1925 all the livestock in Arizona, the cattle and sheep, became infected with "scabbies"
from cattle brought in from Mexico. There was
a quarantine, and for several years, before any
Arizona livestock could be marketed, they had
to be dipped and inspected by government men.
Emory was in charge of building dipping
compounds all over the Reservation. This consisted of a trough made of cement seventy-five
feet long and five feet deep (for sheep), deep

enough to completely cover the animal as it swam through the chemical bath; much water and a boiler for heating it, and coal and wood for fuel were found on the premises. A series of a half dozen pens had gates leading from each pen to the final pen whose exit was into and through the vat. On the day appointed the shepherd drove his sheep to the dipping area and put them in a pen, when available. A herd was dipped and moved out and other individual flocks were moved from pen to pen and finally to the dipping vat.

On hand to inspect and direct the proceedings were the government stockman and veterinarian. When a boiler of water was heated the vet would measure the Black Leaf 40 (germ killer) and give the "go-ahead" word. At intervals he would check the bath and add water and chemicals, while the sheep were held up. Sheep would carry out a lot of water in their wool; a little would drain back, but the water had to be continually replenished. Owners paid two cents per head toward the cost.

The nearest dipping place was at Sand Springs about ten miles below the ranch, where, along with our Navajo neighbors, we had to dip our sheep. Nearly every time there was trouble. One time there were about fifty Navajos and only two Hopi families at the dipping. Lawrence, my brother, was young and strong.

He saw a Navajo slyly opening the gate and letting a few of our sheep in with his flock.
Lawrence jumped to head him off and was
promptly set upon by two Navajos. Lawrence
grabbed one of his adversaries by the arms and
threw him over his head, and then a second and
a third lay in a heap. When they got up, it developed that the government stockman was at
the bottom of the heap and was the last to get
to his feet. Lawrence was unaware that he had
thrown the stockman.

About the same time, Emory jumped to
another gate where a second Navajo was pulling
the same trick, and two Navajos pounced upon
him. Emory says, "I blocked the gate with one
hand while I held the one man by his hair knot
with the other. My sister, Hazel, about sixteen
years old, now came into the fray; climbing
through the barbed wire fence she grabbed the
second man by his hair knot and held him help-
less. He tried to shake her loose but she held on
with a vim. The fence was high and one of my
opponents caught in the barbed wire as I moved
him along, cutting his mouth and making it
bigger."

I was there busy around the fire preparing
food for the men when the commotion drew my
attention. I saw my nephew wrestling with a
Navajo, one trying to open the gate and the
other struggling to keep it closed. I saw two of

our sheep slip through the gate and mix with those of the Navajo in the other pen. I grabbed some good-sized rocks and threw them; one landed squarely in the middle of the back of the Navajo, who looked sheepishly in my direction. (It was the grandfather of Milton, my adopted Navajo son.)

We always lost some sheep at dipping time, driving away with a few less than we came with while someone else drove away with a few more than he brought. But our Navajo neighbors didn't hold hard feelings. When things quieted down, Emory announced, "The food is ready; those who are hungry, come and eat." Believe it or not, those who had been fighting with us came and ate. We fed about fifty people. At last we concluded: This isn't getting us anywhere, fighting. So we decided to try kindness. Destroy your enemy by making him your friend. It worked.

Once a skin disease came to our village. Everyone had it. Some said it was the "seven-year itch." It was all over the state. I have wondered if the germ was not a cousin to the one that gave the cattle the "scabbies." The doctors prescribed the cure; everyone was to come to the school and have a complete bath in water in which there was the same old Black Leaf 40. They had bathtubs and plenty of water. The school children were treated first at school. We went voluntarily on the appointed day, and so did a few others, and had our germ-killer bath in a tub in private.

The majority of the people of the village rebelled and flatly refused to comply. Unless everyone went, the skin infection could not be wiped out. The Health Department prepared to enforce the order. Emory was sent to Keams Canyon to bring back four big steel water troughs. Two of these were put on opposite sides of the school house and filled with water and Black Leaf 40, one side for the men and the other for the women. Then the word went out that unless everyone came in voluntarily, "they" were coming the next day to take them to the dip. On the appointed day, all the rebels gathered at the house of the Chief.

I saw the police as they passed by my house, about fifteen of them, with clubs in their hands. After finding several houses empty, they asked, "Where is everybody?" and were told, "At the Chief's house." When the officers came to the crowd in the yard I could hear a commotion as orders were given and mass defiance shouted back. The police had to get rough. They used their clubs to make the mob realize they meant business. One man was knocked out for a short time. I could hear the women crying and screaming. I wanted to go and see what was happening but decided it would be best for me to stay away.

The police herded the people out of the village and drove them over to the schoolhouse about one-eighth of a mile away. A wagon was provided so the old women could ride, but everyone else walked. Once there, the men and most of the women took their dip without further resistance. A few women would not budge so the police picked them up one by one screaming and kicking and ducked the women, clothes and all, with much splashing and shouting.

To show their utter scorn, these rebels, feeling that they were enduring persecution for righteousness' sake, sat down in the sand on the way home and in defiance rubbed dirt all over their bodies. This I know for sure: One of my aunts, who was real old, said, "Well, I'm glad they brought me over and gave me this bath. It makes me feel good to have a bath in a lot of water, even if I was forced to do it."

Another woman stopped at my place on her way home and shouted, "Take your children and get out. Go and live with the white people." But my nice old godmother said, "Don't pay any attention to them, Helen. They will treat you better in a little while. They know you didn't have anything to do with it."

The Ranch

EMORY FARMED ON CLAN LAND twelve miles southwest from Hotevilla, where his relatives farmed. For several years we would go and plant in the spring, but we lived in the village, going out occasionally and spending a few days cultivating to keep the weeds down, and then going out to harvest in the fall. For a few years we spent the whole summer at the ranch, moving back to Hotevilla so the children could go to school in the fall. We bought a big hogan from a Navajo for our summer home.

We gradually came to feel that life would be better for us in every way if we lived out at the ranch; we could raise more corn for our growing family, the boys could help with the work, and we would be freer from the criticism of our villagers. In 1935 we moved out for good. We built a two-room rock house, using the hillside for the rear wall. It was a good warm house. The hogan we tore down, and the poles from it went into a corral.

The very first year that we lived at the ranch we planted the orchard. The agency brought in little trees, and we bought apples, pears, peaches, plums, and grapevines to plant. From any big peaches we might have, we planted the stones. Soon Emory enlarged on his farming operations, going three miles down the wash where he cleared and planted forty acres more, mostly to corn.

Our ranch was right on the border of the Hopi-Navajo Reservations. There had always been animosity between the people of these tribes, and we had lots of trouble with our Navajo neighbors. The wagon road that the Navajos traveled going to Oraibi to trade passed right by our garden, and many times they stopped and helped themselves to the melons, fruits, and vegetables. If they traveled on horseback their trail passed right in front of our house, and nothing was safe. We sometimes went into the village for a few days and on our return we would find the door broken in, food taken, and things generally scattered about. How could we remedy this? We decided we had to do something about it. It would be best to make friends with those who passed our way. We said to them, "If you are hungry and you find us gone, you are welcome to use the stove to cook your food. If you are cold, come in and make a fire and get warm. If you are tired, you may rest in our beds (they nearly always carried their own blankets). But when you go, please leave things as you found them, and leave the door closed and let us be friends." It worked. Once Emory was asked, "Did you ever find anyone in your bed?" His immediate response was, "Yes, and it wasn't Goldilocks."

There were good ones among our Navajo neighbors. It was the bad ones that gave us the trouble. The honest ones came to trade their meat for our melons and fruit. Once when we were away, a certain Navajo man came, left some meat, took some of our garden stuff, and left a note saying he had taken what he thought was a fair trade. It was, and I always respected that man.

In 1933, the Indian Department began a project for developing and improving water for livestock on both the Hopi and Navajo Reservations. Some sixty or more wells were drilled.

Emory was in charge of setting up the wind-mills and tanks and building cement troughs at each windmill. This work lasted more than three years. Many of the workers were Navajos who could not speak English, so Emory learned the Navajo language. He would be gone all week and come home for Saturday and Sunday. The older boys were big enough by then to do a lot of the home chores.

At one time Emory criticized the department for some new policy they were starting. He was told, "You can't do that when you work for the government." Emory said, "Then I won't work for the government. What is best for my people means a lot more to me than a job." After about a week they sent word, "Come on back. We can't find anyone to take your place."

When the water development was finished, Emory spent all of his time working at the ranch and didn't try to get another job. We had about six hundred head of sheep. My father had his sheep out there too, and he stayed with us some of the time. My brothers Henry and Lawrence were in with my father on the sheep. The pasture was good. We had a few goats with our sheep until the government said, "You can't have goats with your sheep." They took our goats and slaughtered them and took the meat into the village and gave it to those who had no meat.

Emory had a brother who had cattle on the Oraibi range. There was a severe drought and the cattle were dying. When his wife died, the brother was so discouraged and unhappy that he left everything and went to Tuba City. He told Emory that he could have the cattle. Emory sold most of the starving herd to a buyer for a very small price and bought a pair of mules which he gave to his brother. The few cows that were in a little better shape, Emory kept and brought out to our range where the feed was better. That was our start; from that we grew into the cattle business.

For a while we had both sheep and cattle. The children tended the sheep, and the grown-ups looked after the cattle and farming. Then a government decree came that the range was overstocked. Each man was allotted thirty units of livestock. One cow equals one unit. Five sheep equals one unit. We were told we must not keep both sheep and cattle on the same range. We decided to keep the cattle, and my brothers sold their sheep and got cattle and shared the range and the work. However, we kept a few sheep around for mutton and wool.

Wayne recalls:

Once when I was about ten years old, my brother Emory (six) and I were herding the sheep while the folks were harvesting the corn down at the field. We drove the sheep to water around noon and then corraled them near the house. Next we went to the house to get something to eat. The door was locked so we pried a board off a broken window pane and I pushed Emory through, hoping that he could open the door from the inside, but he couldn't, so I made myself smaller and managed to squeeze through the window, too.

Once inside we hunted around and found some bread and several eggs. We made a fire in the wood-burning stove and proceeded to scramble the eggs in the frying pan. When we were about ready to eat we heard horses approaching. They stopped by the house and we could hear a party of Navajos as they dismounted — three or four men and a woman and a girl.

We were scared. We grabbed our pan of scrambled eggs and, holding it between us, pressed ourselves hard against the wall under the window where we had made our entrance. We heard steps come to the door. Pressing harder against the wall, we watched the doorknob turning, but the door wouldn't open. Then we heard steps going away from the house, but someone walked around the house again. Next thing, we saw a knife rip through the screen that covered a little ventilation opening and a long arm reach toward two new coils of rope that were hanging from the ceiling beam. We were scared to death, but we couldn't see our new rope stolen. We shouted and yelled as loud as we could. I grabbed a stick of wood and, reaching as high as I could, struck at the arm. Now we heard retreating footsteps.

We crawled out as fast as we could; I bravely pushed Emory out first, just in time to see the Navajos galloping away. We ran to the sheep and found two lambs outside the pen. We felt sure we had scared the marauders away just in time to save those two sheep from being stolen. When our excitement had subsided a little we crawled back through the window and finally devoured our scrambled eggs and bread before taking the sheep out to graze for the afternoon.

After many years of patience and long suffering, the enmity between ourselves and our relatives and neighbors has at last almost melted away. There is still some jealousy, mostly because our children did well at school, and we worked together and lived better. We were as stubborn about going back to the old ways as they were about changing their ways. A spirit of tolerance has gradually replaced the spirit of hostility.

There were years of good rains, and the grass was good for the livestock; we raised good crops and harvested wagon loads of corn, pumpkins, beans, and melons. When our orchard began bearing fruit, our apples were not wormy, and we harvested them by the wagonload and sold them in the village.

Sweet corn was planted early, to be ready to bake in the pit during the latter part of August or early September. The baking pit was dug on a hillside near the cornfield, eight to nine feet deep, six feet in diameter at the bottom and tapering up to the top to make the opening about two and one half feet in diameter. A ditch was dug from the outside to the bottom of the pit with a six-inch diameter hole to make a draft. Dried greasewood in quantity was gathered days beforehand. The fire in the pit was started early in the morning. An older man watched the fire all day long, adding fuel through the top to keep the fire going, but letting it burn all the wood, not leaving any charcoal.

In the meantime, a party of men, boys and girls, relatives and friends, whoever wanted to help, went to the field to gather the sweet corn, while the women stayed at the house to prepare food for the workers. The ears of corn were pulled from the stalk and loaded into the wagon. If one should find smut on an ear of corn, the boys and girls would chase each other to smear the black dust on each other's faces, and have a good time. When all the corn was gathered, the girls and children would ride with the corn, to the pit, the boys and men following on foot. After the corn was unloaded at the pit, piki and melon were served as a snack to tide the workers over until later.

By late afternoon the pit would be red hot. Water would then be sprinkled over the pile of corn to create more steam (husks were left on the corn while it was cooked). A little of this raw corn was chewed by the girls and blown over the pile, to make the corn sweeter. An ear of corn was placed at the edge of the pit on each of the four directions and simultaneously pushed in. Then everybody would get busy throwing in the pile of corn. Men and boys took turns tromping as the corn neared the top, so that it would be packed down and more corn could go in. A big flat rock would be placed over the opening and a thick layer of husks put around and over the edges of the rock to keep the sand out; then it would be covered well with dry sand to seal. The draft hole was also sealed. Now — everyone was ready to enjoy the feast that the women had ready.

An older man usually slept at the pit to check once in a while for escaping steam. A wet spot of sand would indicate escaping steam, and this would be remedied. Emory's godfather often did this in early years.

At the house, after eating, the men and boys

would go rabbit hunting while the women and girls cleaned up the dishes and visited. The hunting party would come back with several rabbits to be cleaned and cut up and put to roast along with more corn on the outside grill. After all this exercise, everyone would be hungry again. After eating, all would go to bed for a well-earned rest.

In'olden days, and in my early lifetime, the harvesting and all aspects of life had religious significance. Emory's godfather observed this at the corn bake. He watched the morning star, and when it was in the right position, it was time to open the pit. While the steam poured out, he called loudly to the gods and their spirits to come and partake of this food, repeating the invitation four times — from the east, the south, the west, and the north. Being spirits, the gods eat of the vapor from the corn. In the early morning hours we could hear Emory's godfather from the house a mile away. Then he rested or slept while the pit cooled off.

At dawn everybody would get up to go to the pit. Coats and blankets were taken, as it was cold. The baked corn would be taken out, first with a pitchfork. Later when the corn was cooler, the men would take turns going into the pit and handing it up in baskets or buckets until all was taken out. The rest of the party did the husking; they put the corn on a canvas or blanket spread on the ground.

If the corn was well baked it would be brown, otherwise it would be lighter. As the first ears were opened, everyone would be reminded of a story of long ago. It was said that the corn was light when the pit was opened up. The housewife had anticipated nice brown corn. She was so angry at her husband for doing such a poor job that she threw him out and told him to go home to his mother. Even today, each time a bake is on, the host is teased, and if the corn isn't good and brown, they say, "You will have to go home to your mother."

Everyone ate all the corn he wanted as he worked, and he also put aside a few good ears, leaving the husks on to keep it moist, to take home. They teased each other about eating longer ears because the shorter ones have better flavor. Another story is: The woman wanted the longer ears to store, so she suggested, "Eat the shorter ones; they taste better."

The ears were taken to the house to be hung up to dry in the sun. A hole was made in the stock of each ear, and yucca strips were used to string them, a dozen or more on a string which was tied to be hung out to dry. In olden days, the bone from a sheep leg was sharpened and used as an awl for punching the hole. Now we use a nail or an ice pick. After work was done, each family was given some baked corn and some green corn, and they went on their way home.

At the time of the big harvest in the fall we would send word to our neighbors, and they would bring their blankets and come and stay several days, helping to bring in the matured and ripened field corn. The stocks were chopped and brought to the ranch in a wagon each day. Some of the men worked at the field, while the rest sat around the big pile as it was brought in, husking and spreading the ears out to dry on the flat roofs. If there was more corn than the roofs would contain, the men might spread the corn on the sand. When it was thoroughly dry, the corn was stored inside.

The fodder was put away in the shed or on top of it to be used as winter feed for horses and cattle. After each day's work, we would have a corn roast. We would have butchered a sheep or a cow for this occasion. We always planted some late corn so we could have roasting corn until frost.

For the corn roast, first a big fire was made and let to burn down to coals. The corn was shucked, with the stock left on as a handle. The meat had already been cut into suitable pieces. Ribs lent themselves well to this manner of cooking. One or more persons would sit putting on the corn and meat, watching and turning frequently until each piece was cooked on all sides. When a piece was done, it was laid to one side of the grill to be picked up and eaten. This continued until everyone had his fill. Some fruit or melons topped off the meal. Everyone enjoyed sitting around the fire visiting.

Every year we had a day or two of branding. We always had quite a "to do" then. Our relatives and friends came to help with the work, and we would have a fine time feasting and working and visiting again. Of course, when our neighbors were harvesting or branding and needed help, we were always glad to go and help them.

There was always plenty of work to do at the ranch. Emory was lean and muscular, and hard work made him feel good. I was pretty strong too. Emory was kept busy shearing and lambing the sheep, rounding up and branding the cattle, and working the farmland.

The boys helped when they were home in the summertime. They had learned to do their share when they were little and were willing and hard workers. When the cattle were sold, some of the money would go to help with the expense of the boys' education.

We always had to pump water by hand for the sheep. Sometimes after working all day, the boys would say, "We are too tired to pump the water." I would say, "Let's all go and make pumping the water a game. We have to do it, you know."

The children played together and needed no other playmates. When he had time, their father would sometimes take the older boys out and teach them how to make Hopi playthings and play with them or hunt birds' nests. I would play ball with them too.

Edward, our youngest, was born after we moved out to the ranch. When he was five years old he was the only child left at home. There were many days when Edward and myself were the only ones to take the sheep out. It warms my heart to remember how Edward wanted to take care of me. He would walk ahead and say, "You walk here and be careful that the rocks don't hurt your feet, and don't fall." Or he would find a nice place where we could sit down and rest. Toward evening when his little feet got cold he would cry and I might send him on home alone. One time I left the sheep and took Edward on home. They didn't come on in, and even though it was after dark when Emory got home he had to go and bring them in.

When he was only five, Edward would ride on a horse all day with his father, looking after the cattle. Sometimes after such a day we would find him outside playing in the dark with his little cars.

When Wayne was twelve years old, while we were still living in Hotevilla, he reacted positively to a tuberculosis test given at the school. They sent him to a sanitarium in Winslow, Arizona, where he stayed for two years. The last year he was permitted to go to school, but lived in the sanitarium. When he was released, we sent him to Phoenix. We thought the warm winters would benefit his health. He lived with his Aunt Elsie James (Emory's sister) and has never lived on the Reservation since that time.

Eugene was fourteen years of age the first winter we lived at the ranch. He had the responsibility of driving his younger brothers and sister the twelve miles into school at Oraibi, in an old Ford car over country roads in all kinds of weather. That was too expensive. The next year the children stayed in Oraibi in the school dormitories. Emory would take them in on Monday morning in the truck, in time for school; he would also take milk and eggs and any other produce we might have for sale. Since our milk and eggs were not inspected, we could not sell them at the store, but we had plenty of customers among the villagers and teachers. Then again when Emory went after the children on Friday afternoon, he took our surplus produce to sell.

One Friday the roads were wet, and the truck got stuck in the mud. It was about 10:00 p.m. before Emory gave up and they all started walking. Allison, only seven, had to trudge along with her brothers, tired and cold and hungy, while Emory carried Abbott (crippled with arthritis) on his back. It was past midnight when they got home.

Several times we were snowbound for a week or more, but our corn bins were full; there were rabbits to be killed and a sheep to butcher; we had lots of beans and jars of fruit and vegetables, so we didn't mind.

There was the time when the older children were all staying in the dormitory in town. Edward and Marlene were with us at the ranch, too little to go to school. Emory was going to be away for two weeks, and we needed a herder for the sheep, so we rode twelve miles to where a Navajo family was living, to get a herder. Milton, eight years old, volunteered, and a few days later his father brought him to the ranch. He cared for the sheep while Emory was gone. We took him back home and paid his parents for his services.

Some time later Milton came back. He had walked and run the twelve miles and came in at about five in the afternoon, exhausted. I fed him and put him to bed. In a little while, Milton's father came riding up on horseback. He said that Milton had run away several times, but they had followed him and taken him back each time, but today he got up early and no one knew he was gone for a long time, so he came all the way. His father said that Milton was unhappy at home, wouldn't work and wanted to come back to our place. Could he leave him with us? Maybe in a little while he would be ready to come on back home. Milton stayed.

I waited, expecting him to say he wanted to go home, but he never said it. He stayed on and on, was a good worker, and especially good with the stock. Marlene and Edward were younger, but the three were good pals. Soon Edward and Marlene were talking Navajo with Milton. Emory could speak Navajo too, which left me out of the conversation for a time, until Milton learned some Hopi.

Milton had never been to school. The Navajos used their children to herd the sheep, and since they moved about wherever the grass was good, the school men often missed them, and they escaped being taken to school. When it was time we took the children, including Milton, into Oraibi to enroll them in school. The principal would not let Milton enroll, so he herded our sheep that first year. The next winter there was another principal, and he let Milton go to school. Milton was almost ten and big for a first grader. The Hopi boys did not accept him, and he had to fight his way. Milton was a good fighter, and once when they ganged up on him he knocked them right and left. If one tried to pick a fight he would say, "How old are you? I won't fight with a boy who is younger than I am." When the teacher asked Milton a question that he didn't understand, Edward acted as interpreter. Pretty soon Milton learned to speak English and discarded his own language.

Come summer, Milton's father rode over and said to Milton, "Your brothers are all home from school now. Why don't you come home and see your brothers?" He didn't want to go and said, "Why don't they come here and see me? I like it here. I like to eat three times a day. Sometimes we don't eat over there." Milton was finally persuaded to go for a visit, but when he left he said to me, "In not too many days from now you come and bring me something to eat." He stayed at home for two weeks and then came back to us for good. He was one of the family. He called my brothers "Uncle Henry" and "Uncle Lawrence" just the same as Marlene and Edward did. My father was with us then. He was old and nearly blind, and Milton would lead him around carefully, calling him "Grandfather."

In due time Milton went away to school but spent his summers with us. He was five years in Provo, Utah, with a Mormon family. He graduated from high school there at the age of twenty-one years. He learned to play the piano and sing beautifully. You should hear him sing

Indian Love Call. He is good-natured and gets along well with people.

Since his father's death, Milton takes care of his mother's flocks and herds. He is the most dependable and responsible one of the family. Quite often he brings his mother and comes to visit us. She always shows love and gratitude for us all. I call him "my son" and say, "Now Milton, be sure that you don't drink or smoke. You want to get ahead. You know what drinking will do for you." He answers, "I will remember. I'm not that weak." Milton's father had three wives — sisters — and their family is numerous. For a time they prospered, but when the father became a drunkard his affairs suffered.

On stormy days at the ranch, Milton paced the floor restlessly, saying, "We ought to go out and check the range. The cattle are bunched up in the snow, and those Navajos are maybe out there now killing one of our calves. This is just the kind of weather for that. All Navajos are stealers."

In 1946 Emory Jr. was going to Phoenix High School. He worked after school hours in the dairy at the Indian School. There he bought a newborn Holstein heifer. When she was three weeks old we came down in the truck to get her, taking her back to the ranch in a little crate that we made. Edward and Marlene bottle-fed and played with her while she was in the crate for a few days. They named her Daisy.

We put Daisy with the sheep, and she grew up with them, going out to graze in the morning and leading them back at night, with the young herder bringing up the rear. One November night when we came back from the village, we found the sheep not in yet. The herder had abandoned them and gone to town. Emory went out to look for them, but he gave up the search until the next morning. Then about a mile from the ranch he found Daisy with the herd all bunched up together on a little mesa that had three quite steep sides. Daisy's tracks showed that she had walked back and forth all night holding the sheep. A bobcat had come up the far side during the night and had taken a lamb. Daisy was glad to lead the sheep in, and Emory followed.

Emory was asked, "So you think Daisy is smarter than most cows?" He answered, "She is smarter than most people."

She was always a sort of scavenger, eating things that cows don't eat. She would eat the clothes off the clothes line and enjoyed the fine cottons and silk, especially nylon stockings — but she rejected the woolens. Marlene's grandmother gave her a pretty silk dress, but Daisy ate it the first time I washed it and hung it out to dry. I was embarrassed to know what to answer when Grandma kept asking, "Why doesn't Marlene wear the dress that I gave her?" I couldn't say, "Daisy ate it." I beat Daisy at this game by putting the clothes line on top of the flat roof of the house. She would stand gazing longingly up at the line of clothes. This scavenger trait was at last Daisy's undoing. She ate a feed bag made of heavy paper and covered with I don't know what— and died in the spring of 1961. We couldn't eat Daisy.

We always kept a few chickens. Then we decided to go into the chicken business as a way of bringing in more cash. We built good houses for them and kept them clean and had no diseases. We would order baby chicks from Phoenix, a hundred at a time. I would sleep with the new chicks for the first few nights. When the hens began laying we would take a case of eggs and a dozen fryers into Oraibi once a week and sell them at the trading post, the school kitchen, and the Teacher's Club. We raised our chicken feed and bought only laying mash. This netted us around thirty dollars a week. We had a car by then.

Emory and I wanted our children to go to school. No matter what happened, they must have an education. We talked about it, and they were enthusiastic and wanted to do it themselves. Wayne led out and set a good example, although he was a sickly child and was never

very strong until he was in his teens. We worked
and sacrificed to that purpose. We still raised
our food; besides corn we had meat and fruit and
vegetables and eggs and milk (after Daisy). We
lived well and were always healthy. Our neighbors spent their money for bread and foods in
cans at the store and bought ice cream and pop.
They didn't spend time grinding corn and preparing food like their parents before them did.

Wayne and Eugene went to Phoenix Indian
School where they had board and room free,
but when they went into high school they found
they were not qualified to do the work; their
training had not been up to standard, so we sent
the other children to regular public schools.
Each one worked at whatever jobs he could find
to do after school and on Saturday for money
to buy his own clothes and other expenses.

Emory's sister, Elsie James, was a matron
in the dormitories at Phoenix Indian School.
She has been a second mother to my children.
She took them into her home, each in turn after
they had completed the course offered at Oraibi.
Wayne lived with Aunt Elsie from the time he
was in his early teens. Eugene, Emory Jr., and
Allison each stayed with her while going to high
school and junior college in Phoenix.

In 1957 my children were all away in school.
My brother Lawrence was working in Flagstaff,
when I heard about a Hopi woman who was

working in Flagstaff, doing housework. She had a little boy about five years old. At first she hired a sitter to take care of him, but her wages wouldn't pay for it so she would lock him in the room and try to come back to him at noon when she could.

I said I would be glad to take care of the boy. Here on the ranch would be an ideal place for him. He would be company for me when I was by myself. The mother was glad, and Lawrence brought Lorin with him the next time he came. The mother said she would pay me, although I didn't ask for it. For a few months she sent five dollars a week. After about a year we heard that she had married, so I expected her to take Lorin back any time. She wrote me and said she had planned to take him but would I keep him a little longer.

When he was old enough I put Lorin in school at Oraibi. The mother kept saying that maybe she could take Lorin back sometime. It went on and on. After about five years she wrote, "I have given up ever having Lorin back. I would rather you keep him than my people because I know what kind of a home he is in. I have to give him up so you take him."

We speak to Lorin now and then about his mother. We wanted to make a good boy out of him. When he first came I said, "You can call me grandmother or aunt — whatever you want." He said, "I will call you mother and I will call the old man father because I have never had a father and I will really like to have him be my father." To the child, my husband, Emory, seemed like an old man; but to me, Emory is not old. When Lorin's mother gave him up, I had him baptized into the Latter Day Saints Church, the same as I did my own son, Edward. Lorin is a good boy.

In 1954 I went to Phoenix to make a home for the children who were going to school there — Leroy, Allison, Edward, Marlene, and Lorin. We frequently boarded some Hopi student who seemed to show promise. I was in Phoenix six winters. I found some work as housemaid to bring in some money. Emory worked at the trading post in Oraibi, commuting from the ranch every day to care for the livestock. Being able to speak Navajo helped him in the store.

In 1960, Leroy graduated from Arizona State University at Tempe, and Marlene from Central High School. Allison went to Brigham Young University in Provo, Utah, and I went back to the ranch. Edward lived with Wayne in Phoenix and finished Central High School, and Lorin was in Oraibi until he finished eighth grade.

We were so far out at the ranch that I made my own medicine and could cure the children's ills pretty well. These were remedies used by the mothers before me, from what elements were at hand.

Salve for sores: Mix clean white pine pitch with warm mutton tallow. Keep in a jar. It healed up their sores.

For colds: I used a root medicine which the Navajos brought in to trade. It was like Mentholatum, strong and penetrating when held in the mouth, or in the nose. They got it in Oak Creek Canyon.

Abcess or boil: Clean it well with soap and water. Use a sterilized needle, and when the attention of the child is drawn away, split it open. Put clear pitch in at first. It hurts. Then the salve and in a few days it will be well.

For sore eyes: A little salt dissolved in water. Drop it in three times a day.

Leg ache at night: Bathe in hot cedar water.

For stubborn running sores: Rabbit skin burned to a powder; use the ashes left after the burning.

For cough: Boil pitch water. Drink the water now and then during the day. Also rub on chest.

Once my niece, about six years old, at Hotevilla, fell from the terrace down to the garden and crushed her ankle; gangrene set in. The doc-

tor wanted to take her to the hospital and ampu-
tate. He said she would surely die if the leg was
not amputated. Her parents would not consent
but insisted she be left with them to care for.
The foot and leg were swollen and running pus.
Her father washed the foot in hot juniper water.
He burned pumpkin seeds until they were black,
then crushed them into a fine powder and mixed
it with clean white pitch. He made a lot of it and
spread it thick all over the foot. It looked hope-
less. The father fixed fresh medicine every morning, taking off the old poultice and putting on
the new.

After a week it was all black and she seemed
about to die. She wouldn't eat. Then her appe-
tite came back and her leg looked better. The
field nurse came to see her every day and was
astounded. After many weeks of this treatment
the child finally got so she could walk, even
though her foot was a little crooked.

My sister had an abcess, or whatever it is —
a lump, or gathered breast. I nursed her young
baby. The breast was so badly swollen that it
broke open and was very painful. There was a
four-inch hole and you could see cavities and
milk veins all filled with pus. Her husband got
prickly pear cactus fresh every day. He would
hold it near the fire and burn off the thorns, then
split it open. Inside, it was gooey and sticky.
After washing the breast in cedar water and dry-

ing it off he put the cactus over the hole and wrapped the whole breast with cloth all around the body. Every morning he repeated the process with fresh cactus. Every morning it looked clean and better. It took a long time. As the hole got smaller he got a smaller leaf. This man was not a medicine man, but understood the medicinal value of the native herbs and plants.

In 1951 the Hopi Tribal Council was activated. They kept after Emory about the law and order set up. They needed people to act as tribal judges in their courts. In 1953 Emory accepted a tribal judgeship. The Council nominates, subject to the approval of the Superintendent. They operate under the federal code and certain ordinances that have been passed. So long as they act under the federal code the action must be approved by the Superintendent. It is from a sense of duty and public service that he serves. It gives him satisfaction to help administer justice among his own people. He goes from the ranch into Keams Canyon two times each week to hold court. His pay would hardly cover his gasoline cost.

My Church

ONCE THE PEOPLE LIVED in the underworld. The time came when so many of them were wicked that the leaders of those who were good held a council and decided to find another place to live. First, they must find a way out. They planted pine trees, hoping the trees would grow up and pierce the roof. The pine trees grew up to the roof but then bent over and spread. Then the people planted sharp pointed reeds. These grew tall and pierced the sky.

The next thing was to find a place to live. Little hummingbirds were sent up. They flew up and up, circling around the tall reeds, and resting upon them when tired, but finally they fell back down, exhausted. A chicken hawk was sent up next. He could fly better than the little hummingbirds, but after circling higher and higher, he fell back down. One more bird was sent, a catbird that flew with a jerky motion. He reached the top and flew out of the hole, and came to Oraibi. There he found a red-headed ghost, who asked his mission. The bird told his story and asked permission for the people to come up and live there. The ghost consented, and the bird flew back to the underworld and delivered the message.

While the others were busy dancing and merrymaking, the good chiefs and their families hurried to the tall reeds and began to climb. In this they were aided by the god of hard substances who made the reeds firm. Each night they sealed off the reeds to keep from falling back while they slept — hence the joints in the reeds. Finally, all the good people had climbed up through the hole in the sky. One chief watched to keep the bad ones from coming out. When he saw two of these climbing up he shook the reed and dropped them back down and then stopped up the hole.

Arriving in the upper world they found

there was utter darkness. The council attempted
to create light. They took a round piece of buckskin that they had brought with them, took bits
out of the hearts of all people, birds, and beasts,
and placing them in a circle, told it to give light.
No light came. Next they took some white cloth
and cut out a circle onto which they put the bits
from all hearts and put it in the east where it
became the sun. Thus, we have the sun giving
light to everything, and everything welcomes
the sun as it rises.

Now the people headed east for Oraibi. On
the way the little daughter of the Chief died.
This was a great shock and disappointment to
all, because they had thought to leave death
behind them; some evil one must have sneaked
up the reed unnoticed and brought the seeds of
death. The Chief called the people together to
ascertain the guilty party. He made a ball of
sacred cornmeal and tossed it into the air. The
one upon whose head it fell would be the guilty
one. It fell on the head of a maiden. The Chief
was going to throw this one back through the
hole into the underworld. She said, "All right,
it will be as you say, but before you destroy me,
come, I want to show you something." Leading
the way to the opening into the underworld, she
pointed down. When the Chief looked he saw
his daughter playing happily with other children. Thus they learned that you must pass

from this world to achieve immortality. The maiden was spared.

The Chief called upon the mockingbird to give each clan a language written on a piece of stone. Of the two sons of the Chief, the older one received the first language, which is the language of the white man. The younger, the Oraibi Chief, received the Hopi language.

Each clan went in a different direction, taking ears of corn with them brought from the underworld, which would provide food in any land. As they traveled they would stop and plant corn and wait for it to grow so they could harvest and have food; then they would proceed on their journey.

The Chief told his older son to go to the East where the sun rises, and live there with his people. This is the origin of the white man. The younger brother was to live in Oraibi. He was to send for his older brother in time of trouble. If the older brother should ever come and find the Oraibi people backsliding into their old ways, or departing from the traditions, he should cut off the head of the Oraibi Chief and this would end the trouble. The time will come when the white chief brother will come and bring peace and right living.

During the long winter months the Hopi men spend time in the kivas where the older ones repeat the story of the advent of the Hopi and many other legends to the younger men. These are told in allegory form and not told to the women and children. I have learned a lot about these stories from my father and the other men of my family.

The month of December is sacred and special. However, the time is not counted by the calendar but from new moon to new moon. They watch for the little line in the sky that marks the beginning. During this moon there must be an atmosphere of quiet and reverence and prayerfulness throughout the village; none must forget to keep this sacred moon. There has been a time of preparation. There must be no chopping of wood because it makes noise; wood enough to last a month has been chopped and piled near the house. No digging to disturb the earth. No parching or grinding of corn, and no one speaks loudly or shouts, and even the children should be quiet in their play. If you must go outside the house after dark, you should take a little ashes from the fireplace and mark your face with it to ward off the spirit of death who is hovering about and might take you, especially if you have not observed to do all these things.

This time is set apart for teaching the young. The uncles (mother's brothers) go to the homes of their sisters in the evening to teach her children. An uncle is treated with respect, and the family gathers around to listen as he tells about the advent of the Hopi, recites traditions and prophecies, and give instructions. We call it "Pbutsquani" which is like the Ten Commandments. Besides the universal laws as given in the Ten Commandments, he says:

Don't add to the already heavy burden of the sun by causing him to have to awaken you; get up before he does.

Don't be lazy; don't lie in bed after sunup.

When you get up, first thing, run out into the cold air to the water and dash in with your naked body.

Don't eat or drink hot stuff.

Keeping your body cold will make it strong so you can resist disease.

Be industrious.

Be courageous.

Keep your mind clean.

By keeping these commandments you will be ready to meet your white brother when he comes from the East to destroy the wicked ones, and he will not destroy you. The destruction will be so terrible that you might just die of a heart attack from seeing it, unless you are strong and good.

The rule for the girls and women is to get up early and go outside and breathe the fresh air for a little while, and then get morning exercise from grinding corn to be ready to feed the men when they come in.

I can distinctly picture our family in Old Oraibi when I was a little girl, all sitting around the fireplace, with the light from the fire on our faces as we listened to our uncles' voices. I would get so sleepy I thought I could not stand it, as they talked on and on, but if my head nodded, someone would punch me and tell me to listen. I remember the teachings though. Repetition served then as now in remembering. Even as we rode the donkeys going home from Keams Canyon that first time, our fathers repeated these things as they walked along. I think they were troubled because we had missed out on them, being gone those four years.

One special night in December, the night for the storyteller, I looked forward to. A good storyteller would be invited to come and tell the stories that go with the traditions. There would be special refreshments, and we liked it. The people usually planned weddings so they would not be in progress during this time. If one were not finished, the bride would go home, and all activities were suspended during the sacred moon, after which the weaving would continue until all was completed.

Most Hopi boys are good little boys because they know that if they are not, the ogre, whose

diet is bad little boys, will surely come for them
sometime. On a day set, this ogre makes a visit
to the village. Parents who have unruly little
boys "fix it" with the ogre, telling him of the
naughty things that the boy does, to make it
real and "do him good." Children know the day
is coming and are told, "If you are good he won't
come to our house." But everyone is filled with
suspense and fear when the ogre is seen coming into the village, accompanied by a woman
kachina, with a burden basket on her back in
which to carry away the meat for the ogre's supper, and a man kachina, who besides having a
burden basket also has in his hands a big butcher
knife and a meat saw, both blood-stained. They
all look fierce and strike terror into the children's
hearts.

When the ogre comes to the door it is opened
by the father, who comes out to meet him. The
little boy, shaking in his boots, stands between
his father and mother, and the ogre inquires:

"Does Chono live here?"

"Yes, he lives here. Here he is. He is our
little boy."

"He is a bad little boy. I have come to get
him. I want him for my supper."

"We love him. We don't think he is that bad.
What has he done?"

Then Ogre recites in detail why Chono
should become a meal for him. All during this

time the room is filled with shrieks and howls initiated by grandpa and grandma and taken up loudly by Chono and his brothers and sisters. Father and mother plead eloquently the defense and finally offer some meat, say a hind quarter of fresh mutton with corn and piki thrown in for good measure in exchange for their little boy. Finally, Ogre admits that he likes little boys best but agrees to accept the offered exchange, on condition that Chono will confess his sins and promise not to do it any more, which Chono is only too willing to do. Mother brings out the food, which had been made ready beforehand, and puts it in the burden basket, and all are relieved as the ogre passes on to another house, later to be seen departing from the village with baskets filled with meat and other food.

One evening in Hotevilla they were having a sort of mixed dance just for entertainment, where miscellaneous kachinas participate. I left Eugene home because he was too little, but took Wayne, four, with me. I was late and so was sitting on the front row in the kiva. I wasn't paying much attention as the ogre came looking around wanting one of the bad children for his supper. As he passed by he grabbed Wayne so quickly that I hardly realized what was happening. I snatched him back and began talking. You had to be a good talker and quick. I said Wayne wasn't a bad boy; he had always been meek and good. But the ogre insisted. Wayne was scared to death and crying. All the women were sorry for him. As a last resort, I handed Wayne to a woman sitting behind me, and she and the other women hid him with their skirts and shawls while I hurried home and gathered some bread and mutton and a jar of jam. Then after speeding back, I put the food into the ogre's burden basket and said, "Here, you take this. You will like this better than Wayne." So I had the last word. Poor little Wayne went to see the dance just once, and the ogre had to seize upon him.

Whenever an uncle comes to visit, little Hopi boys are as good as they can be, because the uncle is the official disciplinarian of his nephews the year round. When the first car came through Hotevilla, it must have been in the early 1930's. The streets were narrow and sandy, and the car went real slow through the village. All the children came running to see the automobile. Some of the boys, including Wayne and Eugene, hung onto the car, pushing and running. My brother Henry saw them and told them sharply to stop, that they might get hurt; but they didn't heed him. Henry took off his belt and gave each of them a few lashes. This was his privilege and duty.

One Hopi ceremony re-enacts the confusion

of tongues at the Tower of Babel. We were in Hotevilla two times during this performance. It is done during the night. Those men not eligible to participate, and the women and children of the village were not allowed to stay in their own homes if they lived close to certain kivas, but had to go to the other end of the village and spend the night with relatives or friends. I was curious and didn't go to sleep. I could hear the tinkle of tiny bells, then big bells, and then the tramping of many feet as the performers came together in the middle of the night. You never heard anything more confusing; all talking at the top of their voices; none speaking their own tongue, but rather making a babble of sound, yelling loudly. Certainly a dramatic reproduction of the Tower of Babel.

While the ritual part of the Hopi religion had no appeal to me — it was crude — the things my parents taught me about the way to live were good. When we were living in Hotevilla, my father was often in our home. During the long winter evenings he would explain the teachings of the kiva saying, "You are young now and may not be interested, but I must teach you now while I am here with you. As you grow older, then you will learn to understand and know it is the truth." This has come to pass.

He said:

The white man has kept a written record of the history of the people from the beginning, while the Hopis have passed their history from one generation to another by word of mouth. With the telling over the years, some of it has been omitted or misunderstood, and changes have been made. The written record is more accurate and true. There will come a time when the written record will be brought to the Hopis by the white man. There will be many religions taught. You will need to be wise to recognize and choose the right church. It will teach you to be humble and will not try to force you into it. When that time comes we should all forsake our native religion and join this true church. There will come a time when all the people of the earth will belong to the one true church, and we will all speak the same language and be as one people.

He said this many times, and at the end he would say, "I tell you this because you are my own blood. I want you to take it to heart and teach it to your children. I want you and your children to live by those teachings and benefit by what I have said."

Both Emory and I heard him say this long

before we ever heard of the *Book of Mormon*. He *did* say it in our presence. The Traditionals would now deny that this is what their fathers used to teach. When we heard of and read the *Book of Mormon* it sounded like a familiar story. Reading the *Bible* and the *Book of Mormon* has helped us to understand the Hopi traditions, and the Hopi traditions help us to understand these books of scripture.

My father admonished me not to indulge in gossip about or with my neighbors. "Never go visiting just to gossip. Some women are just made to gossip. It is the work of the devil." Some of his sayings follow:

If someone does you wrong, do not try to pay him back and get revenge; rather be humble and feel in your heart, "Some day I will do something good for that person," and do it.

Any time you have more than others — more blessings — you should share. Whenever you see other people suffering want, if you have something give them some.

In times past the Hopis had talents which they have lost through sin, but these talents will come back through righteous living.

Whatever work you are doing, work hard.

The Hopi language will be the universal language some day.

The redheaded ghost is Satan. He was already on earth when the first people came.

During the 1860's and 1870's, Jacob Hamblin led several scouting parties of Mormons to the Hopi villages, their object being to make friends and to teach their religion. This was the very first contact that the Hopis had with this religious group. Of course, this was before my time, but I do remember hearing my elders talk of "Jee-co-ba." There are still a few of the ancient ones who remember and tell of Jacob, his policy of honesty and kindness, in contrast to the abuse and exploitation they had known at the hands of the other *pahanas* who had come.

On one of his trips, Jacob took Tuba, one of the chief men of Oraibi, and his wife Talasnimka — she was known as kachina mana, girl kachina — back to Utah with him where they stayed for a year. It was a goodwill trip; they left in the fall of 1871 and returned in September, 1872. Tuba's wife was my grandmother's sister. She came back wearing a cotton dress and a bonnet and, like Marco Polo, she brought back "things" — yeast, a coffeepot, a dishpan, and a dutch oven. One of the first of the wagons of the settlers to Arizona passed by Oraibi and in it was a cookstove for Talasnimka. It was the very first stove in Oraibi. As a little girl I remember being fascinated with the tiny door that had a slide in it to make a draft. I also remember my great aunt in her old age. After the death of her husband, Tuba, she lived in Bacabi with some of her nieces and later in a little house that was built there for her.

The Hopis always classed the Mormons as different and separate from other whites, especially after Tuba's visit to Utah. They felt that the Mormons were friendly and did not look down on the Indians. They were industrious and would share their food with hungry Indians. The Hopis said, "When we go to their homes they invite us in to sit at the table and eat with them. They do not give us food on a plate to eat outside like dogs."

There is a bone in the neck of the sheep that looks like a hat. That bone is called "mo mon a" or Mormon. We recognized Mormons afar because they wore hats. The first dolls brought in by the trader were called "Mo-mon-ho-ya," or little Mormon.

One afternoon in the 1920's a man drove into Hotevilla and parked his car in my neighbor's yard. He was a stranger and didn't look like a government worker. It was getting late, and he was still sitting in his car; no one had offered him hospitality; they wouldn't ask anybody in. So

I went over and asked if he wanted to stay in the village overnight and if he was hungry. He said he had come on a mission to make friends with the Hopi tribe. He accepted my invitation and came over to my house and ate supper and spent the evening with us. He slept in his car, as I had a big family to sleep.

He told me that he was a Mormon Elder and was thankful to be invited into our house since no one else seemed to want him. He had come to see the Chief and find out if the church could open a mission there. He chopped wood for me. I understood that he stayed in the village for a week. We had been in the village taking care of peaches and went back to the ranch the next morning. I never learned if he made a good impression on the Chief.

It was in 1950 that I next heard of the Mormons. Abbott was staying with Aunt Elsie, beginning his first year at Phoenix Union High School, when he was suddenly stricken with acute arthritis. He was in great pain and unable to move. They carried him out on a stretcher and took him home to Elsie. He was in hospitals in Phoenix and Winslow, bedfast for a year. After three years he was released from hospitals but was rigid from the waist down. Wayne took his books on radar to him, and Abbott learned how to repair radios by studying while he was in bed. He wrote home about some Mormon

Elders coming to visit him in the hospital. He said, "Here is a religion we should get interested in and try to learn more about." Of course I wanted to do what Abbott wanted because he had been sick so much, and I went along with him.

Once when one of my babies was born, I was in Hotevilla, when quite a crowd of Mormons from around "Joe" City and Snowflake came there. They called the people together in front of the store and talked to us, giving us a sermon. I listened with interest, but none of them ever came back again for a long time. The first full-time missionaries came to Oraibi in 1951. The first ones to come to our house were Brother Virgil Bushman and his wife Ruth.

Emory Jr. had come home from West Point, having been given a medical discharge after being there for a few months. He was very disappointed and discouraged but had decided that he wanted to go to college and was considering the Brigham Young University at Provo, Utah. I don't know how they found it out, but the Bushmans drove out to the ranch one day. They stayed with me all day until Emory Jr. came in from riding the range. Brother Bushman rode a horse with Emory all the next day and talked him into going to Brigham Young University. Emory left right away.

Virgil and Ruth Bushman then started com-

ing out regularly once a week teaching Emory,
Abbott, and me the Gospel in a systematic way.
What they taught sounded good to me, like a
familiar philosophy, like the teachings we were
used to, like the Hopi way. I was really converted the first week and believed everything,
although I was not baptized right soon. I read
the *Book of Mormon*. It sounded exactly like
Hopi tradition.

When the young missionaries first came to
Hotevilla they had a hard time. A villager would
see them coming and go from door to door saying, "Don't let them in. Don't listen to them."
When I saw the doors slammed in the faces of
the missionaries, I felt like it was slammed in
my face even before I became interested. So I
often invited them to my house to eat and sleep,
and they were happy to accept. Emory and I
sometimes went with them to visit the Navajos,
and he acted as their interpreter.

When the Mormon missionaries came to
Second Mesa, they taught the first chapters of
the *Book of Mormon*, telling of a prophet named
Lehi who was told by the Lord to take his family, a wife and four sons, and leave Jerusalem
because that city was going to be destroyed
because of the wickedness of the inhabitants
(this in the year 600 B.C.), how they journeyed
many days in the wilderness on their way to the
sea, how Lehi sent his sons back to Jerusalem

to get their records of their forefathers and the teachings of their prophets, how they were led to a land that was choice above all other lands, having crossed the mighty waters and landed in America.

The head priests of the Hopis at Second Mesa, hearing these things, accosted the Elders and angrily said, "How come you know these things? You are not old enough to know it. Who told you these things? Only older men, high in the priesthood, know that. You keep your mouths shut."

My son Wayne was living in Phoenix, and he had been converted and baptized into the Church of Jesus Christ of Latter Day Saints, commonly called "Mormons." I felt that I should go ahead and be baptized and that I wanted my son to baptize me. I went to Phoenix to attend Allison's graduation from high school in May, 1953. While there, I told the Bishop I wanted to be baptized by my son Wayne, which event transpired on May 3, 1953. Edward and Marlene were baptized at the same time. I have no doubt I did right. I have never been sorry. It has made a better woman of me, and I have surely been happy in my church. I have had great satisfaction working in the church, even though it seemed like everything was against me at times.

The women's organization of the Mormon

Church is known as the Relief Society. When the Bushmans were missionaries in Oraibi, Sister Bushman held Relief Society meetings in her home. Quite a few women came. They also held Relief Society meetings and Sunday School in Hotevilla some of the time. I went whenever I could. It is my nature to like to help people who are in need or sick or poor or hungry. I love to relieve them. The Relief Society helped show me how. Once I had washed and ironed some clothes for a woman who was sick. When I went to deliver them her little boy — the rascal — said, "You look like a witch." Emory said, "She is one of the best witches we have. Always helping people."

I always went to Relief Society meetings while I was in Phoenix. I enjoyed the lessons given by the women who were born in the church. I sang with the Singing Mothers group, singing alto in some classical numbers.

I have done everything I could to get the Hopi women interested in Relief Society work. I had to take the whole responsibility most of the time. I would ride into the village with Emory on the days he went to Keams Canyon to hold court, and hold meetings in the different homes of whatever place was available, and I had a good group. We liked to sing the songs I had learned. I would give a short lesson, and then we worked. Quilt making was a year-round project. We pieced tops from scraps of this and that and got our linings here and there. For our filling, there was wool from the sheep that we could wash and card, or we could buy a cotton batt from the Sears Roebuck catalog, if we had the money. The quilting bee was a good place to promote friendliness. In time each one would receive a nice quilt all had helped make.

In harvest season we worked together as a part of Relief Society, canning and bottling fruit. I brought my pressure cooker so we could put up vegetables and meats. I had a sealer, and we bought cans in lots of a thousand from Sears. Our crowning effort was a bazaar in Oraibi, where we made one hundred and fifty dollars.

Dasube

DASUBE (*daw* — accent on this syllable — *su be* — easy on the *be*) is a Hopi word that means the rosy light that glows in the western sky after sundown and continues on even into the night.

The ranch is my home and I love it. I hope I can live here always. I can't imagine myself living any other place. Most people who are as old as Emory and I have better houses and furniture than we do. We sacrificed so we could invest our money in our children. However, lately we are living in a four-room cinder-block house, financed by our sons. My brothers, Henry and Lawrence, who are good builders, did the construction work during the time when they were not employed in Winslow or Flagstaff or on the Reservation. Henry said, "You have always been like our own mother and we do this for you." I cook with "bu" gas and have a gas refrigerator. It is all nice, but the love that goes with it is the best part.

The years have passed by with cycles of planting and cultivating the corn and other crops, and then the harvest. The days have brought their routine tasks — cooking, sewing, cleaning, and helping with the outside work when necessary. It has been real living and never monotonous. Our family increased in its own time and rhythm. We had ten babies in all (plus two foster sons — Milton and Lorin). Each child brought with it its own welcome and place, and increased the love in the group.

When I think upon my children and the kind of people that they are, a feeling of joy and pride fills my heart, and I say to myself, "I have had a good life." While it has taken more pages telling of my childhood, school days, and marriage, those years were only laying the foundation for wifehood and motherhood — the best years of my life, the real living. All my life I have liked to work, and I have accomplished a lot

in my lifetime, raising food, making clothes for
the children, nearly everything they had at first,
and all the other tasks that go into the making
of a home.

Most of my chums gave up and went back
to their Hopi ways when they returned home
from school. They gave in when their parents
urged them to forget what they had learned,
although they admit that many of the ways of the
pahana are better. I was stubborn and held on
and would not give up, even though my sister
was continuously trying to discourage me, even
urged me to quit reading. After being away
for so long I was not used to the old kind of life
and could not be happy living as the others did.
My children would not be what they are, or
doing the things they are doing, if I had forsaken the good that I learned at school. We
chose the good from both ways of living.

For many years there was no change in my
father's attitude. He remained Hostile and
showed in some ways his disapproval of me, and
he could not bring himself to admit that some of
the education was good. In his later life though,
he said several times, "You are a good daughter.
You have good children. You raise a lot of food
and take care of it and feed us good and never
waste a thing." And finally he did tell me, "I
marvel at the way you stood up against all the
people, and we have all lived better because of

it." When my sister's husband died my father said to me, "I would like to spend the rest of my life with you, but it is my duty to care for Verlie until she marries again." He would come back and live with us for periods of time, but he wanted to be sure that he died in Verlie's house; he wanted to be sure of a traditional Hopi burial. He didn't want his body buried in a box. Even though he was ninety years of age when he died in 1955, he was never senile but was wise to the end of his days.

To his grandsons he advised, "You of the younger generation, stand for what is right. Go to school and be diligent, don't play around, but learn the white man's language and his ways so you can come back and help your people and fight the *pahana* in his own way. Who knows? It might be one of you to save our land. The Navajos are living on our land and keep encroaching farther. We must get them off. It is our land and we must have it. It will be a ticklish job to get our land away from the Navajos. It will take men of courage and patience and integrity and other virtues to stand up to them. Get an order from the government and do it in a legal way and don't give up.

"Don't be lazy. Work hard. Pretty soon I will leave you. If you do this, before I am gone too long maybe each one of you will have a car. Always remember this: No one lives on his own power. In and of ourselves we are nothing. There is a higher power that helps us."

I was very fortunate in my marriage to a man like Emory. We were meant for each other. God has something to do with it. If I had had the other kind of husband, I could not have had a good family. We have had a good life together. My husband likes to have things done right. If I did silly things when I was young, he would reprove me in a nice way. He is kind and considerate.

I don't get angry quickly. We have hardly ever quarreled but waited until we got over being mad at each other, after we relaxed a little, and then talked things over and settled our differences. We have tried not to argue before our children. Sometimes I felt sorry for them when their father punished them, but I never interfered. I used to work so hard, sometimes being up all night with them, I would be so tired, but now that they are all grown and I look back it doesn't seem so hard, and I wish I had them back again.

I never curl my hair or use make-up or anything to improve my looks. My mother's admonition is behind all this. Even when I was a little girl she would tell me not to use any artificial stuff on my face, that it is always best and more honest to look the way you really are. Besides, your skin will grow old faster if you use the white man's cosmetics and then stop using them. I must have taken it to heart, because my conscience bothered me whenever I did succumb and use a little lipstick. When she came to visit me in Keams Canyon, my mother would bring me a fresh supply of very fine blue cornmeal. I would rub it on my face after I washed it, to take away the shininess. The little oil in the cornmeal made the skin feel smooth and silky.

In Retrospect

LOUISE UDALL died February 14, 1974, at her home in Phoenix. At the funeral services in the Ninth Ward Chapel of the Church of Jesus Christ of the Latter-Day Saints, Helen Seka-quaptewa gave the following eulogy on her friend of many years:

I am honored to be a part of this occasion. Louise has been an important part of my life the past seventeen years. She has shared my family and my home as I have hers.

Some of the most intimate times, and those most revealing of her character, took place on the Hopi Reservation in and around our home. I would like to remember the best of those times and share them with you today.

Louise was a lover of people. She had the quality in her to accept everyone for himself. She made each of us whose life she touched feel important and needed. Her ways were excellent and pleasant. Our activities led us to many gatherings and community doings. Wherever we went, she never questioned or shied away from strange customs or foods. She always enjoyed herself and relished the food set before her. If weary, she would lie down on anything handy, whether it was a couch or a sheepskin. Her manners so pleased the hosts that I often heard this comment in the Hopi language: "What kind of Pahaana (white person) is this? She does not feel ill at ease; she is one of us." She was easily accepted by all we met. Many happy times did we have with groups of women in just these ways. I must not overlook the fact that she perked up our spirits by giving inspirational talks at our church meetings each time she came to Hopiland.

I met Louise for the first time at a Relief Society workday meeting on the Maricopa Reservation. We did not become fully acquainted with each other until sometime later when she asked me to help her with the church women's group there. I worked with her four winter seasons. When she was to leave there, one of the speakers said something like this: "We thank you for your love and patience, giving us yourself, and teaching us many things to do with our hands. Your services will be cherished and will be like an echo for many years to come." Louise liked the poetry of this statement.

She did not like to put things off. If there was a good intention in her mind, she would do it "right now, or [as she said] the spirit will die and never be activated." This brings to my mind her ever-ready sewing kit and button box. She often replaced or mended a missing button or torn shirt or dress during the course of visits to my many relatives. Her industry and homemaking talents would not allow her hands to be idle, and she even taught little girls to crochet.

Best of all, she was a part of my family; a second mother and grandmother to my posterity. She told me I am the same to hers, for which I am honored. We took pride in our children and agreed privately with each other that we would stand in each other's stead where they were concerned.

We never argued. Not that we did not have differences, but we agreed that it was a waste of time and might spoil our friendship. As it turned out, we had more in common than not.

She created work for me while I lived in Phoenix—ironing once a week so we could spend the day together. She did not really need any help and I knew this, but she knew that I had a houseful of boys to feed, so she saw to it that she and her family were kept cleaned and pressed for the sake of our friendship and my boys' well-being. During those times, we talked and sang more than we did anything else.

At the close of my remembrances, I want to recall Louise as she was in my home. I remember how much she enjoyed being a part of the daily life: the corn shelling, the quilting, the corn roasts, the harvesting. I have keen recollections of Louise on horseback, or climbing the mesas nearby; of the storytelling and funny incidents shared as we sat around the open fire evenings during the corn roasting season. We shared so many such days together that I cannot remember them all for this time. But this was the Louise Udall we knew and loved.

EMORY SEKAQUAPTEWA JR., reflected in 1969 on his parents, Helen and Emory, and on the years of his growing up. His cherished memories of family closeness and strength will help readers to appreciate Louise Udall's devotion to the entire household during the years of her friendship with Helen:

I can't help having a feeling of love and deep respect for my parents when I realize what a terrific uphill battle they waged just to provide the bare necessities of life. Every one of us had to work to get the job done. When I was very young I came to realize that rain was the key to the harvest and to our livelihood. The hope and prayer for rain was always in everyone's mind. In thinking about this, I sensed what my parents must have been thinking too, and I was compelled to try hard every day, which brought a feeling of contentment at the end of the day. Each one of us did his best and thereby learned to endure and take whatever life meted out. Hard work is the key to life; nature's forces may work against you, but if you attune your life to nature she will work in your favor. I learned to choose the good from the bad in everything.

Seeing the long-suffering and patience displayed by my parents, very early I developed a feeling of confidence and security in them. I thought that my father was capable of being President of the United States, and that my mother could stand by his side in any situation. Now in my more mature years, my childhood estimate still stands, has even increased because of my better understanding of life.

INDEX

Abbott, Sarah, 145, 146, 165, 191
Advent, Hopi, 224, 227
Albert, Amelia, 128
Anderson, Mr., 163

baby ashes, 180
Bacabi, 34, 152
baptize, 23, 242
Bean Dance, 23
Beecho, 6
Bible, 17, 236
bone dolls, 15, 101, 107
borrowed wife, 119
branding, 209
Breid, Dr. Jacob, 33, 133, 134, 167, 170, 171
Brigham Young University, 240
Brown, Supt. John B., 130, 133, 135, 139, 140, 142
Bushman, Virgil, 240
    Ruth, 240

Carlisle Institute, 30, 87, 154
Catholic priests, 21, 46
children, 188, 220
Chosnysie, 35
Christmas, 14, 33, 102
cisterns, 21
clan land, 197
Commandments, Ten, 229
corn bake, 204
    roast, 208
Crane, Leo, 133

Daisy, 215, 218
death, 148
December, 228
Dirkson, Rev., 163
Dowawisnima, 7

Ella Ghost, 126
Epp, Rev., 71, 73, 74, 78

father, death, 6, 10, 248
    teachings, 234, 235, 236, 247
Flagstaff, 57, 175, 176
Fort Huachuca, 87, 97, 99
freighting, 176
Friendlies, 13, 14, 74, 75, 76, 77, 78

Gannett, Ed, 71, 84
Gates, Gertrude, 71, 78, 84
godfather, 27, 152
godmother, 24, 25, 101
Goldilocks, 199

hair washing, 155, 156, 164, 206
Hamblin, Jacob, 237
harvest, 208
Hazel, 193
Health Department, 195
Henry, 10, 56, 76, 175, 246
hide and seek, 8
Hill, Edna, 191
Home Dance, 66, 108, 165
Hostiles, 8, 13, 14, 30, 64, 66, 67, 69, 70, 77, 78, 94, 100, 107, 121, 139
Hotevilla, 36, 115, 121, 143, 152, 167, 186, 197
Hotevilla springs, 22, 76, 80
Hubbell, Lorenzo, Jr., 102, 175, 191

Idaho, 167
immortality, 227

James, Aunt Elsie, 211, 218, 239

kachina, 5, 20, 23, 24, 25, 26
kachinvaki, 23, 24
Keams Canyon, 31, 86, 91, 92
Keith, Miltona, 72, 73, 78, 84
Kiakochomovi, 22, 89
kiva, 4, 25

Lapwai, 167, 170, 173
Lawrence, 123, 147, 148, 175,
    192, 200, 218, 246
Lemmon, Supt., 68, 70, 80, 81,
    85, 86, 88, 91
Leupp, Commissioner, 72, 84
Line, the, 83
Lololama, 63, 64, 65
Lorin, 219, 220

Marriage, 119, 153
mata, 109, 110
matate, 109, 110
medicines, 221
Mennonites, 14, 71, 163
Milton, 194, 213, 214, 215
Moenkopi, 37, 46
Mormon, Book of, 236
Mormons, 37, 238, 239, 240, 241
mother (Sehynim), 6, 123, 147

Navajo, 94, 96, 198, 203
Navajo police, 8, 11, 12
New Oraibi, 22, 89

ogre, 231
Old Oraibi, 6, 7, 14, 22, 68
Oraibi Wash, 38

pahana, 237, 247, 248
Phoenix Indian School, 35, 132
piki, 112, 113
piki cupboard, 9
police, 8, 130

Qumanimka, 6

rabbit blanket, 9
Relief Society, 243
Rincon, 76, 148
Riverside, 33

San Francisco Peaks, 23, 66
Sand Springs, 192
Satan, 237
scabbies, 191, 194
school, 8
Scott, Mrs., 139
Sehynim, 6
Sekaquaptewa, Abbott, 188, 212,
    239, 241
    Allison, 188
    Edward, 188, 210
    Emory, Sr., 10, 30, 61, 134,
        140, 152
    Emory, Jr., 215, 240
    Eugene, 188, 211
    LeRoy, 188
    Joy, 162, 178, 174
    Marlene, 188, 212
    Selwyn, 188
    Wayne, 115, 140, 185, 190,
        201, 211, 218, 232, 239
Selema, Robert, 83
sex, 117
Sherman Institute, 88
Shungopovi, 65, 71, 74
Stanley, Elizabeth, 12, 72, 73,
    74, 78, 84
Story Teller, 230
Sunday School, 14, 129, 135
Susie, 34, 152, 154, 155, 156,
    165, 174

Talashongnewa, Sam, 6, 100,
    247, 248, 234, 235, 236, 247
Talasnimka, 238
Tewaquaptewa, 45, 65, 67, 68,
    71, 72, 74, 75, 78, 79, 80,
    88, 89, 90
"They," 13, 82, 129, 195
Tower of Babel, 234
traders, 57, 61
Traditionals, 13, 236
traditions, 122, 227
Tuba, 237, 238
Tuba City, 37

uncle, 228, 230, 233

Verlie, 76, 86, 123, 144, 148,
    151, 154, 156, 222, 248

Well, The, 17
West Point, 115
wife, borrowed, 119

Yokeoma, 45, 64, 65, 68, 71, 73,
    74, 78, 79, 80, 82, 85, 87